ORGANIC Café
COOKBOOK

ORGANIC *Café* COOKBOOK

d&C
David & Charles

To my son Hugo,
whose life inspired both me and my other children,
Nick and Harriet, to create the Organic Café

When we follow our consciences, we obey the laws of nature
Hugo Herbert d:1985

ACKNOWLEDGEMENTS

We are grateful to a large number of people for their enthusiasm, help and support from the early days of running the Organic Café, right through to the production of this book.

Particular thanks go to Lizzie Shawe – one of the best cooks I know – who has worked so hard to build the Organic Café Cookshop and to our 'Queen of Cakes', Anne Dorrington.

To my friend Jane Taylor, without whose generosity the Organic Café would never have got off the ground; to my husband Bryn Jones, for all his encouragement and for putting his hand into his pocket when he knew it would clean him out; and to all the chefs and staff who have helped to create the Organic Café concept, espe-cially our inspired Head Chef Issa Cissokho, Paul Oraha, Simon Prest, Juliet Greener, Letty Autin, Mary O'Rourke, David Callister, John O'Reilly, Mary Lincoln, Charma Milbourne, Tamsi Beith, Susanne Jackson, Emma Chalmers, Jane Grove, Fernando Rodriguez, Tomas Locker, Terenzia Morgan and C-Jon.

Thank you also to Anna Mumford who asked me to write this book, Michael Whitehead and Robin Whitecross for the design, Mark Williams for his photographs, Susie Hallam for her enthusiasm, Anne Sheasby for unravelling my recipes and everyone at my publishers, David & Charles, who got so firmly behind this book.

As we travel through life, good friends often seem to be the only con-stant. Those who support and love us through the good times and the bad. My love and thanks go to: my terrific children Nick and Harriet, my sister Sally Watson, my brother James Charlton, my brother-in-law Wilfrid Watson, my aunt 'Tommy' Stafford (for those perfect childhood holi-days), Folla Cann, Marina Martin, Agatha Schwager, Olive Wilson, Lucy Goldman, Jane Bourvis, Valerie Smith, Daniel Mankowitz, Katrina Bayonas, Marylin Aslani, Sarah Litvinoff, Joel Adler, and last – but certainly not least – my mother-in-law, Olwen Jones.

I would like to pay special tribute here to Vera Chaney, founder of the Green Network, for her tireless work in promoting awareness of pesticide-related illnesses.

The Organic Café is at 25 Lonsdale Road, London NW6 6RA, the Organic Café Cookshops are at 54 Salusbury Road, London NW6 and 102 Golborne Road, London W10. All telephone enquiries to 020 7372 1232.

A DAVID & CHARLES BOOK

First published in the UK in 1999

Copyright © David & Charles 1999
Text copyright © Carol Charlton 1999

A catalogue record for this book is available from the British Library.

ISBN 0 7153 0940 4

Photographs © Mark Williams 1999, (except page 146 Adam Brett, pages 19 (bottom), 20, 21, 22, 23, 26, 32, 52, 54, 72, 80, 83, 84 (bottom), 100, 108, 152, 153, 172 (top right, middle left, bottom centre), 178-79, 181 and 184 Polly Farquharson, page 1 Paul Harmer, page 105 St Helena Fisheries Corporation, page 147 Adrian Weinbrecht, page 127 Whole Earth Foods, and pages 11 and 81 Elizabeth Zeschin.

Carol Charlton has asserted her right to be identified as author of this work in accordance with the Copyright, Designs and Patents Act, 1988. All rights reserved. No part of this publication may be reproduced, stored in a retrieval system, or transmitted, in any form or by any means, electronic or mechanical, by photocopying, recording or otherwise, with-out prior permission in writing from the publisher.

Art editors: Michael Whitehead and Robin Whitecross
Cookery editor: Anne Sheasby
Printed in the UK by Butler & Tanner Limited, Frome for David & Charles
Brunel House   Newton Abbot   Devon

Contents

Where did it all start? Was it my mother's soft fruit garden and her mouth-melting pastry, the larder lined with jars of home-made lemon curd, jams and pickles or that first intoxicating sip of home-made elderflower wine? My earliest memories are of food — very often the lack of it, for I was a 'war baby' and we were strictly rationed. But we were luckier than most as my mother kept her suburban garden like a small-holding. Chickens roosted in the Bramley apple tree to grace our table on special occasions, and most of our vegetables were home-grown.

When I was seventeen, my mother found me climbing out of my bedroom window into the arms of a jazz trumpeter. 'You marry him or you go to France', she stormed. I went to France. To Dijon in the heart of Burgundy country to be precise. Here, I flirted with French philosophy and French men. But mostly I learned to cook, with Madame, wife of the famous cheesemaker, M. Rouy, in a large house with stone-flagged floors and an abundant cellar. Each day the younger son and I were sent to tap off wine from vast barrels or to cut portions from the large wheels of Rouy brie and camembert, so that they could warm and melt in time for dinner. It was a complete revelation to me — both the long hours we spent preparing food and the utter bliss that accompanied every meal. After the culinary desert of post-war Britain, this was a glimpse of heaven.

Back in London, it was now the swinging sixties and Elizabeth David had arrived. In my circle of young marrieds, it was *de rigueur* to give at least two dinner parties a week. We experimented with wild duck and grew fat on chocolate mousse.

During the sixties, I divorced and married again to Spanish musician/composer, Carlos

Risueño — we moved with my two children to live in Spain, first in Madrid and then in a small village in the foothills of the Sierra Nevada, in Southern Spain. Here, in the seductive, Moorish province of Granada, where houses still had no running water, we settled to a life of self-sufficiency. We had our own sweet-scented Mediterranean garden in which we grew everything for our table, including rabbits and snails. Our food was geared to the seasons — not just on land but at sea, too. With the children's help — I now had a daughter as well as two sons — I preserved everything in sight from shiny, yellow medlars and wild hare,

Left: Carol Charlton Above: Carol runs the Organic Café with her two children, Nick and Harriet.

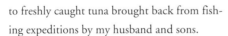

to freshly caught tuna brought back from fishing expeditions by my husband and sons.

Then it was back again to England and now as a full-time working mother the food had to be good and fast. My sister Sally's recipe for goulash made with tomato soup was a great standby. But my time on the continent gave me a different attitude to food and I became increasingly concerned about the British approach, where supermarkets take the place of the vibrant fresh food markets to be found in the rest of the world and the lure of cheap food is used by stores as a marketing tool. In no other European country would parents allow their children to eat what British children eat for lunch. Nowhere else (apart from North America, where the food shocked me) would cheap hot dog, burger and ice cream vans be allowed to park outside school gates and sell their nasty, non-nutritious food to our children. It's a scandal.

In 1985, when my middle son became ill and later died from an obscure cancer of the bone, I gave up my job and went to work for Greenpeace. Here, I was struck by how much effort was being put into saving the environment, but how few questions were being asked about human health, when it seemed to me that the health of both were inextricably linked. My concern was shared by Bryn Jones

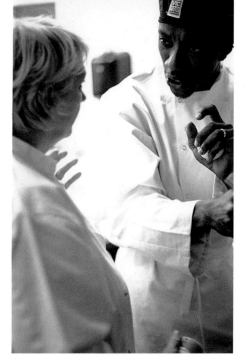

The success of the Organic Café owes much to the enthusiasm and commitment of a dedicated team in both the kitchen and front of house.

who was then the chairman of Greenpeace and we went on to work together on these very issues.

Ten years later, in 1995, when working on a booklet about pesticide-related problems and wondering how I could best use my energies in the next stage of my life, I remembered something my children and I had discussed ten years before – the idea of opening an organic restaurant. Like so many ideas, it had been raised and then faded – justifiably in fact as it would have been very difficult to do in those days. Ten years on, however, we felt it might just be possible to fulfil that idea. So, with very little money, but a great deal of commitment and good friends, the Organic Café began life in 1997 in London's Queens Park.

It is a family affair inspired by our passion for organic food. Having run organic markets, we knew most of the producers of organic food before we started. We also knew that it would be extremely hard work, but we were – and are – totally committed to converting people to organic food. What better way to achieve this than by starting an organic restaurant? Several Organic Café 'angels' helped us with seed funding, time and encouragement. We are thrilled with our success and by the fact that we might help to bring about a shift in the way people think about food – how it is produced and how it affects their own health as well as the health of the environment.

We are a family of foodies and when we lived in Spain – despairing of somewhere to eat out – we started our own seasonal barbecue on the hillside above the village (my boys were waiting tables and washing up from the age of 7). Inspired by our success, we started a more permanent restaurant in an old ice factory. The restaurant business, as my children say, 'is in the blood'. Both my children and I have degrees and previous careers in other areas and my son's MBA has proved invaluable in our expanding business – though the usefulness of my daughter's Russian has yet to become apparent! The first Organic Café was part of our organic market in Camden, North London (alas, no longer) and two brilliant cooks who worked with us there are now producing the food for our Organic Café Cookshop and Deli: Lizzie Shawe and Anne Donnington.

It has been very hard for small organic growers to survive in the last 40 years in a world where farming has become big business and agro-chemicals (such as pesticides and synthetic fertilizers) are subsidized. Smallholdings and family farms have become rare, but the organic movement has fought to maintain traditional and sensitive farming methods, believing in principles that are not just about being organic, but also about maintaining a way of life. Organic farmers are more likely to be compassionate farmers and more likely to care about their animals, their environment and the people who work on the land.

So when you eat organic food, you are not only doing so because it is good for you, you are also helping to support a small group of courageous people – some of whom you will meet in this book – without whom we would still be in the hands of the huge agro-chemical industries and their poisonous products. When we first opened the Café, organic ingredients were not readily available. It is amazing how fast the supply base is growing and by 1997, we were able to buy organic ingredients so comprehensively that we earned certification by the Soil Association. That's progress – real progress!

Opposite: Herb-stuffed, pot-roasted lamb (page 96) with tajine of chicken (page 86) in the background.

storecupboard

Almost all the ingredients we use at the Café are organic, and our commitment to using organic ingredients earned us our official certification by the Soil Association in 1997. When you are cooking at home, however, there is a little more room for flexibility – the balance of organic to non-organic ingredients you use is entirely up to you and a tablespoon of brandy, for example, is not going to change the taste of the dish in any important way. Although organic ingredients are now much more readily available, don't be discouraged from making a dish if you can't find an organic version of some of the minor ingredients but do remember that organic ingredients really do taste different, so aim to buy organic for the major constituents of the recipe.

There are a number of basic ingredients we use at the Café on a daily basis. The choice of these storecupboard essentials is very important and I would like to explain a bit about them in this short round-up.

BREAD AND FLOUR

Most of the bread you buy at the supermarket or your local shop contains chemical improvers, dough-conditioners, additives and artificial flavourings. It is made with flour that has been ground from cereals which are regularly sprayed with at least 20 different pesticides during the growing period, and then even more chemicals are applied after harvesting during the storage period. White flour is very often bleached, too, and is ground with steel mills in such a way as to remove the essential bran and germ which provides fibre, nutrition and flavour.

When you buy organic bread, you are guaranteed organic and pesticide-free ingredients, with no refined white sugar, unhealthy fat or bleaching. Most organic bread is made from stoneground flour using traditional methods so that the nutritional value and flavour is good. It also represents much better value for money than conventional bread – as you can judge when you feel the weight!

BUTTER

We never use margarine or other butter substitute spreads, not just because of the taste, but also because the manufacturing process – hydrogenation – heats the fats to a high temperature to produce something called trans-fatty acids, now believed to be a cause of heart disease. So it seems that it is healthier for your heart to eat butter, after all – and organic butter is irresistible!

CHEESE

Organic cheese is made from organic milk by traditional cheesemakers using rennet – an enzyme that comes from the lining of a calf's stomach – to curdle the milk. Organic cheese uses rennet from organically-reared calves, in the traditional way. Most vegetarian cheeses, however, use a non-animal rennet which is genetically modified. In fact there is only one non-genetically-modified vegetarian rennet and this is made from fungi – it is called microbial rennet. So, if you want to eat vegetarian organic cheese but want to avoid genetically modified ingredients, make sure you check where the rennet came from before buying the cheese.

DRIED FRUIT & NUTS

Most commercial brands of dried fruits and nuts are sprayed with post-harvest preservatives to prolong their shelf life. These conventional mixes may also contain some or most of the following: non-organic fruit glucose syrup, salt, glazing agents, vegetable oil, glycerine, potassium sorbate, sulphur dioxide and tartaric acid and this is all coated with a non-vegetable oil.

You can now buy a full range of organic dried fruit and nuts with no such additives.

EGGS

Organic eggs are produced by hens fed on organic food, and reared in a humane way without use of antibiotics, growth promoters or yolk colourants. Organic eggs are all free-range. Scandalously, however, most of the non-organic 'free-range' eggs sold in the supermarkets, heavily promoted with pictures of open fields and blue skies, are actually intensively farmed – the chickens are reared in huge flocks inside crowded barns with only limited access to the outside world. Don't buy them.

Note that the eggs used in the recipes in this book are all medium-sized unless otherwise stated.

FROZEN FOODS

It is always assumed that frozen food is less nutritious than fresh, but fresh vegetables quickly begin to lose their vitamins once they are picked. So, in fact, eating vegetables that are frozen

soon after being picked is much better for you than eating 'fresh' vegetables that have been stored unfrozen for more than four days. A wide range of organic frozen vegetables is now available.

HONEY

Bees cover a wide area in their search for flowers from which to gather nectar, so honey is one of the more difficult foods for which to gain organic certification. However, there are some organically certified honeys. We use a wild organic honey from Zambia. It comes from bees that live in the tropical forests in an area that has been inspected by the Soil Association to ensure the bees cannot gather nectar from pesticide-treated crops or flowers from the edges of the forest. With the threat of genetically modified crops looming, the health credentials of honeys will be increasingly hard to secure as bees pick up pollen from genetically modified crops and redistribute it to traditional crops as well as bringing it to the honey itself.

JAMS & MARMALADES

As a rule of thumb, fruits are sprayed with pesticides more often than vegetables. Apples receive the biggest dose with as many as 24 different chemicals sprayed on them during their life on the tree – and this does not include post-harvest chemical

treatment to prolong shelf-life. Soft fruit, too, comes in for a hammering. Soft fruit grown for a processing purpose, such as jam, may be sprayed a dozen times while ripening on the branch. This chemically-contaminated fruit is then cooked with white sugar and preservatives to make jam.

Organic jams are made simply with raw sugar, the fruit and a little lemon juice. Natural pectin is added to help the jam set in some cases.

MAYONNAISE & SALAD DRESSINGS

It doesn't take long to make our quick mayo (see page 32), but if you're short of time there are several organic brands made from sunflower oil, egg yolk, vinegar and seasonings. You can also buy organic vinaigrettes and American-style dressings.

MILK AND DAIRY

It is most important to buy organic milk and dairy products not just to avoid pesticide residues but also to avoid BST, a genetically-engineered dairy cow hormone. There is currently a moratorium on the use of BST in Europe until the year 2000, after which the agro-chemical companies who brought us genetically modified seeds are lobbying to introduce the hormone. It will be hard for farmers to resist using it because those who do not use it to increase milk yields will not be able to compete on the open market. We are, in fact, already consuming BST in this country because it is present in a number of American dairy products from ice cream (**not** Ben and Jerry's) to the cheese on pizzas.

MOZZARELLA

The difference between mozzarella made from cow's milk and true mozzarella made with buffalo milk is immense. *Mozzarella di Bufala* is made from the milk of the water buffalo which graze the water meadows along the Latium coast between Rome and Naples. Only one brand of mozzarella is certified organic, but all buffalo mozzarella is traditionally made. Good Italian delicatessens stock it, but take care to eat it fresh!

OILS

Most commercial oils are extracted at high temperatures, a process which destroys or reduces the mineral and vitamin content. Many are then further refined with solvents to produce a lighter colour and taste. Some are then even bleached. Buy extra virgin olive oil, which is produced by a cold pressing method. We use two types of extra virgin olive oil: an estate-bottled organic oil for salads and table breads and a cheaper, well-made, commercial, extra virgin oil for cooking, not yet available as organic. Estate oil tastes of thick, fresh olives and is expensive because

the oil is extracted in the traditional way from hand-picked olives. The modern extraction method used for commercial grade oils can still produce extra virgin or cold pressed oil, but it does affect the thickness and the flavour. However, it is better for cooking as it does not have such a strong taste and so does not overpower other flavours. If you want to reduce the taste of the oil or the amount of oil used still further, try using a mix of half oil and half stock.

PEPPER & OTHER SPICES

This is straightforward. Pepper is now cultivated on a large-scale as a monoculture and sprayed during cultivation and after harvesting, so it is important to buy organic. In traditional forest gardens, peppers grow under the banana trees along with chillis and other spices, not on commercial plantations. A wide range of organic spices are now available through Hambleden Herbs (see page 181).

PRESERVED FOOD

Many organic products are now available in tins and jars. The tomato products are especially good (and this includes ketchups), as are the sugar-free baked beans and the mediterranean vegetable products such as chargrilled aubergines in olive oil. There are also many pâtés and burger mixes. You can even get

organic instant mashed potato. Bottled fruit is usually preserved in a syrup made from water and organic fruit juice.

RICE

Rice is another heavily-sprayed crop which often contains significant pesticide residues. We use a lot of organic brown rice, which I highly recommend. It is a good source of nutrition and has a delightful nutty flavour and chewy texture.

SALT

Table salt is refined, with a processed, bland and boring taste made worse by the magnesium carbonate added to keep it dry and free-flowing. Organic sea salt comes from certified unpolluted sources and is harvested and evaporated using traditional methods. In the Café we use the organically-certified sea salt from the Isle of Anglesey, Wales which is available through mail order (see page 181). Sea salt that is not certified as organic still represents a much healthier option than table salt. It is unwashed, unrefined, sun-dried and contains many minerals. There are many different sea salts, each with a different mineral content and a different taste. The *fleur de sel* from the grey salt beds of Brittany, for instance, retains all its minerals and has a complex, almost sweet flavour. Many people swear by Trapani sea salt which comes from

Sicily, while our own British sea salt from Malden is equally good.

SMOKED FOOD

Wood-smoking is an ancient method of preserving food – the smoke actually halts the process of decay. However, artificial smoked flavourings are often added to some 'smoked' foods which are not really smoked at all. Always insist on natural, wood-smoked produce.

SOYA

You can now find a large number of organic soya products which are made with non-genetically engineered soya. For our soy sauce we use Tamari which is naturally fermented soya. Other soy sauces are fermented using a high heating process, which kills the natural vitamins and minerals.

STOCKS

A good stock really transforms a dish and I have given recipes below for the vegetable and meat stocks that we make in the Café. Obviously, if you are trying to fit good, healthy cooking around a busy life you won't always have time to make stock. The alternative is to use an organic bouillon and there are several good ones on the market. I highly recommend one made by Marigold which is available in most health food shops and supermarkets.

VEGETABLE STOCK

MAKES ABOUT 850ml (1½ pints)

4 onions
2 sticks celery
2 carrots
55g (2oz) butter
1 head garlic, peeled and crushed
1 tablespoon black peppercorns
40g (1½oz) each of chopped fresh
    basil, tarragon and sage

Coarsely chop the onions, celery and carrots. Melt the butter in a large saucepan, add the chopped vegetables, garlic and peppercorns and sauté until the vegetables are soft, stirring occasionally.

Add 1.2 litres (2 pints) cold water, bring to the boil, then reduce the heat and simmer, uncovered, for about 20 minutes. Add the herbs and continue to simmer for a further 5 minutes.

Remove from the heat, allow to cool, then strain through a sieve, reserving the stock and discarding the vegetables and herbs. This stock will keep in a covered container in the refrigerator for about 2 days or in the freezer for up to 3 months.

CHICKEN STOCK

Because we use the breasts of chicken for one dish and the legs for another, we are left with the chicken carcass, wings and giblets, which we make into stock for sauces and gravies.
MAKES ABOUT 1.2 litres (2 pints)

Chop the chicken wings into small pieces and place together with the chicken carcass on a baking tray. Drizzle with a little olive oil and bake in a preheated oven at 190°C/ 375°F/ Gas Mark 5 for about 30 minutes – this will bring out the flavour. In the meantime, prepare the following vegetables as instructed below.

    Wings and carcass of 1 chicken
    2 sticks celery
    2 carrots
    1 large onion
    1 leek, washed
    4 cloves garlic
    giblets of 1 chicken
    2 bay leaves
    1 sprig of fresh thyme
    2 sprigs of fresh parsley

Roughly chop the celery, carrots, onion, leek and garlic and set aside. Remove the chicken carcass and wings from the oven and place in a large saucepan with the giblets. Cover with about 2.8 litres (5 pints) cold water. Add the chopped vegetables and herbs, bring to the boil, then reduce the heat and simmer, uncovered, for about 1 hour.

Remove from the heat and allow to cool, then skim the fat from the top of the liquid and discard the fat. Strain the stock through a fine sieve, reserving the stock and discarding the chicken pieces, vegetables and herbs. This stock will keep in a covered container in the refrigerator for up to 2 days, or in the freezer for up to 3 months.

VEGETABLE STOCK CAKES

In a collection of traditional recipes from Nova Scotia, Canada, comes what is probably the ancestor of the bouillon cube – 'Portable Soup' or 'Pocket Soup'. Here a vegetable stock was slowly simmered for 12 hours, then boiled briskly for 8 more until it became a solid stock. This was then formed into cakes and it was common practice for 'sea-faring men and woodsmen' to carry little cakes in their pockets, adding them to boiling water to obtain an instant broth.

SUGAR

Approximately half the sugar we eat comes from sugar beet – one of the most heavily sprayed crops of all. One of the pesticides used on sugar beet– lindane – has been linked with high rates of breast cancer here and in other parts of the world. Buy organic sugar as a top priority.

SWEETS & SNACKS

You can buy several brands of organic chocolate, sweets, fruit snacks, nut and seed bars and pop-corn. As most conventional crisps or corn chips are made from pesticide-treated crops you should lose no time in switching to organic brands. This is especially important because children tend to eat and drink large quantities of these food-stuffs and so are exposed to greater risks from pesticide residues.

VINEGAR

We use a lot of cider vinegar – I particularly like the taste it gives – and you can also buy organic versions of wine and balsamic vinegars. I am attracted to cider vinegar because it is reputed to have therapeutic qualities. It is also prescribed for weight loss – and did you know that cows with arthritic joints are given cider vinegar? Aspell's cider vinegar is made from whole apples, as opposed to concentrate, and is bottled unpasteurized.

WATER

Your tap water may contain micro-pollutants and metallic contaminants such as aluminium, lead and cadmium. Chlorine is also routinely added to tap water to disinfect it – although it does not kill all disease-causing organisms and may itself be harmful to human health. If you drink tap water, I recommend using a combined activated-carbon/ reverse-osmosis water treatment system.

Fluoride in water is a much debated subject. It is a highly toxic substance and can be harmful even in very small doses, but it is added to drinking water to prevent tooth decay. It is better not to drink fluori-dated water supplies. Check that your water company does not put fluoride in the water – if it does, don't use toothpaste with added fluoride.

When you buy bottled water, choose certified mineral waters, because the source will have been tested for purity. Avoid water in plastic bottles, because impurities from the plastic can leach into the water.

WINE

Pesticide use on non-organic vines is very high and residues of fungicides are frequently found in imported wine samples. Cheap wine has also been laced with a cocktail of chemicals and high levels of sulphur, which is used as a preservative – this is why you can get a headache from non-organic wine.

Organic wine is made from grapes grown without the use of pesticides and artificial fertilizers and uses a traditional copper compound called 'Bordeaux mixture' to protect against mildew. Only very small amounts of sulphur may be added to the wine.

Even at the Organic Café we cannot always obtain organic produce for every recipe – at the time of writing, I cannot find organic lemongrass! So don't despair if you can't find some ingredients. Good-quality organic produce at cheaper prices is becoming more readily available. We simply have to keep insisting on safe organic food for ourselves and our families.

Everyday essentials

In the Café and the Cookshop, we always have essentials to prepare for the day such as breads, pastas and pizzas. We use flour from two organic millers, Doves Farm and Shipton Mill. Doves offer a mail order service, but there are many other small organic millers and there may well be one near you. We buy flour from these mills confident that it is made from grains grown without pesticides, that it is stoneground to preserve maximum flavour and nutrition, and that it is not bleached like conventional flour. Pesticide use on non-organic cereal is high and most grains are also sprayed with chemicals after harvesting to prolong their shelf life.

In fact, we cannot make all our own bread – not with 400 brunches to serve every weekend – so we also buy in bread from Sid Ashton, the Celtic Baker. He is one of the unsung heroes of the organic movement, who rises at 5am every morning to start baking. From a career as a violinist in the Welsh National Orchestra, Sid worked on the night buses to pay his way through university, before setting up his own engineering business. In the 1974 recession, Sid lost everything – and he resolved to make a fresh start. He ended up in retreat in a Welsh cottage, which had a traditional Welsh faggot oven. Bored, Sid decided to restore the oven and start baking. Soon he was supplying all the local shops. Now with a turnover of 2,000 loaves every week, he supplies many high street shops and has his own stalls at London's Spitalfields and Portobello organic markets.

Organic bakers such as Sid of The Celtic Bakery and other pioneers like Andrew Whitley of the Village Bakery in Cumbria are enjoying soaring sales, while sales of cheap, white sliced bread – the product of supermarket mentalities – are declining. It seems that people are discriminating after all and the 'yuck' factor is determining people's choices.

Top: Bread at Spitalfields Organic Market, London. Below: Many organic farms now have shops which stock a range of everyday essentials

SHIPTON MILL

At the end of a winding lane, in a clearing surrounded by fields and woodlands on the banks of a tributary of the River Avon in Gloucestershire, stands a Cotswold stone mill, a record of which goes back to medieval times when the Miller paid rent of 'a quart of good ale and a bushel of flour'. Even older is the process used at the mill to turn grain into flour – grinding between giant round stones. Milling in the traditional way requires skill, time and the best quality ingredients.

It took owner operator John Lister three years to find the perfect milling stones. They were eventually tracked down in the Marne valley in France. These stones produce some of the most nutritious and tasty flour in the world, made in the same way as it was in medieval days. Stonegrinding retains all the goodness of the flour, unlike steel milling where the essential bran and germ is engineered away. Once John had established the finest milling technique, he started to look for better grains, increasingly turning to organic sources.

Above: Shipton Mill has stood on the banks of the River Avon in Gloucestershire, since medieval times.
Below: The wheat used to make bread flour affects the flavour and texture of the finished loaf.

To help John in his search for different grains, he enlisted the help of Dr John Letts of Reading University, whose passion it is to roam the world looking for ancient cereals. One of these – now known as Maris Widgeon – he pulled out of a 300-year old thatched roof in Suffolk. From the few grains taken from one ear of wheat, a local farmer near Shipton Mill now grows enough to be sold commercially. This grain is particularly good in bread-making because of its high gluten content.

Nowadays, non-organic flours are made from only three different wheat grains, compared to the hundreds of varieties used before the war – no wonder our bread is so boring! The wheat you use not only determines the taste of the bread but also greatly affects how the dough behaves and thus its texture. As a general rule of thumb, strong wheat flour is used for bread making, medium for pasta and soft for pastry. By buying flour direct from organic mills, you can experience better tasting bread and restore health and vitality to this essential food.

The other basic ingredients for a dough are yeast to make it rise, sugar to activate the yeast and conserve the bread for longer and salt for taste. Salt also helps to retain moisture and elasticity in the dough. Nothing tastes as good as bread made with traditional yeast (see page 22) but unless breadmaking is your career or your hobby it simply is not a practical option. We buy in a fresh organic yeast which we mix with tepid water and sugar and leave to ferment (froth) in a warm place. This takes about 10 minutes, but care must be taken with the water temperature. If it is too hot it will kill the yeast, but if the water is too cold the yeast will not ferment. For beginners, or people short of time, it best to use a fast-action dried yeast which you just sprinkle into the flour.

Above: Wheat during the milling process at Shipton Mill. Below: Buying organic produce puts shopper and producer in direct contact reforging lost links in the food chain and adding a new and exciting dimension to shopping for food.

BREAD

Even if you can't make your own bread every day there are recipes here which are ideal for weekend brunches, buffets and special occasions.

COUNTRY BREAD

We make country bread every day as our basic bread for toast and sandwiches. Sometimes we add herbs and cheddar cheese for a savoury accompaniment to soups and salads.

MAKES ONE 900g (2lb) LOAF

15g (½oz) fresh yeast or 1 tablespoon dried yeast or 1 sachet fast-action dried yeast
1 tablespoon clear runny honey
300ml (½ pint) warm water
700g (1lb 9oz) strong plain white flour
2 teaspoons sea salt
1 egg, lightly beaten, to glaze

In a small bowl, mix the fresh yeast with the honey and then pour in the warm water. Leave in a warm place to ferment or 'froth' for about 15 minutes (for the dried yeasts, follow manufacturer's instructions). Sift together the flour and salt into a large bowl and make a well in the centre. Pour the yeast mixture into this and mix to a stiffish dough. If the dough is sticky, sprinkle a little more flour onto it until it leaves the sides of the bowl. Form into a ball and tip out onto a floured surface.

Knead until smooth and springy to the touch (see panel opposite) – this will take about 15 minutes. Return the dough to a large,

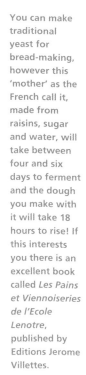

You can make traditional yeast for bread-making, however this 'mother' as the French call it, made from raisins, sugar and water, will take between four and six days to ferment and the dough you make with it will take 18 hours to rise! If this interests you there is an excellent book called *Les Pains et Viennoiseries de l'Ecole Lenotre*, published by Editions Jerome Villettes.

oiled bowl, cover with a damp cloth or cling-film and leave to rise at room temperature until it has more or less doubled in size. This should take at least 1 hour, but don't be tempted to rush this stage as bread that rises too quickly tastes too yeasty.

Lightly grease a baking sheet and set aside. Preheat the oven to 220°C/425°F/Gas Mark 7. When the dough has risen, turn it out onto a floured surface and knead for a further 10 min-utes, knocking out all the air bubbles. Shape the dough into a rough oblong with your hands, score the top and place on the prepared baking sheet. Brush with beaten egg to glaze.

Bake in the oven for 10 minutes, then reduce the oven temperature to 190°C/375°F/Gas Mark 5 and bake for a further 25 minutes or until golden and firm. Remove the bread from the oven and turn it over before returning it to the oven to bake for a further 5 minutes. It should sound hollow when tapped on the underside, if not, put it back in the oven and bake for a further 5 minutes. Place on a wire rack to cool.

BRIOCHE BREAD

Brioche is the most versatile of breads. The loaf is excellent for soft, slightly sweet, buttery sandwiches or to eat with soup. A brioche roll can be used for wrapping sausages, fillet of beef, or sautéed mushrooms. A richer brioche can be achieved by increasing the butter content – some bakers in France match every kilo of flour with one of butter! This can be flavoured with dried fruits or fried to make doughnuts.

MAKES ONE 900g (2lb) LOAF

40g (1½oz) fresh yeast or 3 tablespoons dried yeast or 3 sachets fast-action dried yeast
85g (3oz) brown sugar
4½ tablespoons warm water
700g (1lb 9oz) plain white flour
3 pinches of sea salt
6 eggs, beaten
175g (6oz) butter, melted
beaten egg, to glaze

In a small bowl, blend the yeast with the sugar and warm water until smooth, stirring until the yeast has completely dissolved. Leave in a warm place for about 15 minutes until frothy (for the dried yeasts, follow the manufacturer's instruc-tions). Sift the flour and salt together in a large bowl and make a well in the centre. Add the yeast liquid all at once and mix together with a wooden spoon. Add the beaten eggs and melted butter and work to a soft dough first with the spoon, then with your hands, bringing the dough together in a circular movement. Turn onto a cool, lightly floured surface and knead for about 5 minutes until smooth and elastic. Place in a large, oiled bowl and cover with a warm, damp tea cloth or clingfilm and leave to rise at room temperature until double in size.

Kneading is important for binding the dough and distributing the yeast evenly, so that the bread rises with a close texture. Ideally, kneading is done by hand as yeast loves the warmth. The English and American method is done on a floured board, pushing the dough away with one hand, folding it, turning it and pushing again. But, in France, I have seen it simply being lifted up into the air and thrown down on to the board. Whatever the method, kneading should last several minutes and the finished dough should look smooth and slightly shiny with a characteristic elastic texture.

Left: Fresh focaccia. Before you add the rosemary, you can immerse it in boiling water for 30 seconds then chop it and add it to the dough, this reduces the slight bitterness. Opposite: Harriet with the evening batch of focaccia.

Lightly grease a baking sheet and set aside. Preheat the oven to 200°C/400°F/Gas Mark 6. Lift the dough out of the bowl and back onto a lightly floured surface, knead lightly then shape or plait (by dividing into three lengths, then plaiting together) the dough. Place it on the prepared baking sheet, then brush with beaten egg to glaze and bake in the oven for about 35 minutes until golden brown. Place on a wire rack to cool.

FOCACCIA

We serve this focaccia as our house bread in the evenings accompanied by little dishes of cold-pressed olive oil flavoured with garlic and chillies. With focaccia you can use anything you have to hand to go inside or on top. We generally use olives or home-dried tomatoes and whatever herbs we have, but I have seen a focaccia topped with fresh quartered figs and mozzarella!

MAKES 1 LARGE FOCACCIA LOAF
FOR THE DOUGH:
15g (½oz) fresh yeast or 1 tablespoon dried yeast
    or 1 sachet fast-action dried yeast
225ml (8fl oz) warm water
40g (1½oz) brown sugar
350g (12oz) strong plain white flour
    (or half strong white and half strong wholemeal)
½ teaspoon sea salt

125ml (4fl oz) cold-pressed olive oil
85g (3oz) onions, thinly sliced
1 tablespoon chopped fresh rosemary
8 pitted olives (any colour), chopped
FOR THE TOPPING:
1 tablespoon chopped fresh rosemary
½ teaspoon rock salt
6 oven-dried tomatoes, optional (see page 148)
cold-pressed olive oil, for drizzling

To make the dough, crumble the fresh yeast into a bowl and blend with half the warm water and the sugar. Leave in a warm place for about 15 minutes, until frothy. If using dried or fast-action yeasts follow the manufacturer's instructions.

Pour the flour and sea salt into a mixing bowl and then stir in the yeast mixture. Add the remaining water and olive oil and mix and turn until the dough comes away from the sides of the bowl (the dough should be neither too dry nor too wet). Turn out onto a floured surface and either knead by hand for 10 minutes, or knead in a bowl using an electric mixer fitted with a dough hook for 5 minutes, until smooth and elastic. Knead the sliced onions, chopped olives and chopped rosemary into the dough.

Grease a 24 x 24cm (9½ x 9½in) baking tin with olive oil and press the dough into it with your fingertips, or shape into a round and place on a greased baking tray. Sprinkle the dough with the rosemary and rock salt. If using oven-dried tomatoes, lay these over the dough. Brush or smear some olive oil all over the top. Cover with a warm, damp tea towel or clingfilm and leave to rise at room temperature for 30 minutes.

Preheat the oven to 200°C/400°F/Gas Mark 6. Bake in the oven for 20 minutes, starting with 5 minutes on the top shelf of the oven to colour the bread, then 10 minutes on the middle shelf and 5 minutes on the bottom shelf to settle it. Each time you change the position of the bread in the oven, drizzle a little more oil on the top of the loaf. Place on a wire rack to cool.

FIVE MINUTE FOCACCIA

My great friend Sarah Litvinoff supplied this recipe. She's a busy journalist and one of the best cooks I know. As she has a large extended family always dropping in, she needs to produce good bread, fast, to bulk out impromptu meals.

MAKES ONE 450g (1lb) LOAF

450g (1lb) strong plain white flour

1 sachet fast-action dried yeast

125ml (4fl oz) extra virgin olive oil, plus extra
    for brushing

300ml (½ pint) warm water

sea salt, for sprinkling

TOPPED WITH ANY COMBINATION OF:

– oven-dried or sun dried tomatoes

– pitted olives, green or black or mixed

– artichoke hearts in oil, drained

– thin slices of red onion

Put the flour and yeast in a food processor and blend briefly to mix. With the motor still running, drizzle in the olive oil (you can use the oil from the preserved tomatoes if they have it), then slowly add enough warm water to make a wettish dough.

Grease a baking sheet and spread the dough out on it. It doesn't matter how rough or lumpy it looks – the lumpier the better. Brush with olive oil or smear the oil over the dough with your hands. Sprinkle liberally with sea salt (there's none in the dough so don't be cautious).

Finish with your choice of topping, pressing it down slightly into the dough and then leave to rise at room temperature, covered with a damp tea towel, for about 30 minutes. You'll know it's risen enough when the topping looks nicely bedded down. Bake as directed on previous page in the standard focaccia recipe.

YEAST-FREE YOGHURT AND HERB BREAD

One of our chefs, Juliet, introduced me to this delicious bread and as many people now have a reaction to yeast it is incredibly useful.

MAKES 1 LOAF

    450g (1lb) unbleached plain white flour
    1 teaspoon baking powder
    ¾ teaspoon fine sea salt
    225g (8oz) Greek yoghurt
    5 tablespoons melted butter
    2 large eggs, beaten
    85g (3oz) clear runny honey
    3 tablespoons chopped fresh mixed basil
        and thyme

Preheat the oven to 180°C/350°F/Gas Mark 4. Lightly grease and flour a 20 x 20cm (8 x 8in) baking dish and set aside. Terracotta dishes are good for this bread.

Sift together all the dry ingredients and make a well in the centre. In a separate bowl, mix together the yoghurt, melted butter, eggs, honey and herbs.

Pour the yoghurt mixture into the well in the dry ingredients and mix well. Pour into the prepared dish and bake in the oven for 40-45 minutes. Place on a wire rack and leave to cool for at least 20 minutes before serving.

GLUTEN-FREE MIXED GRAIN BREAD

This recipe was given to me by a French-Canadian friend. It is a perfect antidote to white bread/gluten overdose. There are a lot of different flours involved, but it makes a very tasty bread and freezes beautifully.

MAKES ONE 450g (1lb) LOAF

    140g (5oz) white rice flour
    25g (1oz) brown rice flour
    55g (2oz) chick pea flour
    55g (2oz) tapioca flour
    55g (2oz) potato flour
    25g (1oz) brown sugar
    1 tablespoon xantham gum or cornflour
    1 teaspoon salt
    1 teaspoon fast-action dried yeast
    425ml (¾ pint) warm water
    2 eggs, beaten
    50ml (2fl oz) vegetable oil or melted butter
    1 teaspoon white wine vinegar or lemon juice

Place all the ingredients in a bowl and mix together well. Leave to rise at room temperature for 1 hour, covered with a warm, damp tea towel or cling film.

Grease a 450g (1lb) loaf tin and set aside. Preheat the oven to 220°C/425°F/Gas Mark 7. Turn the mixture onto a floured surface and knead for 10 minutes. Shape the dough and place it in the prepared loaf tin.

Bake in the oven for about 30-40 minutes, then turn out onto a wire rack and leave to cool. When cooled, slice and freeze so that you can use one slice at a time straight from the freezer. For variety, add chopped sun-dried tomatoes, pesto or chopped herbs to the basic mixture.

**Left: A range of interesting flours should be one of the store-cupboard mainstays.
Opposite: Yeast-free Yoghurt and Herb Bread**

ORGANIC CAFÉ BRUSCHETTA AND CROSTINI

It seems odd to use terms such as bruschetta and crostini, when we promote locally grown produce, but, in English, we don't have the words that conjure up the right picture.

Organic Café bruschetta is the Italian version of an open sandwich. Take good, tasty bread, lightly toast or grill it (so the outside is crisp and the inside soft), rub it with garlic, drizzle it with the finest cold-pressed olive oil and top it with anything from the freshest tomatoes and basil to oven-roasted vegetables or soft cheeses sprinkled with herbs and seasoning.

Organic Café crostini are small pieces of bread that are brushed with olive oil and oven toasted until crisp. They make good bite-sized snacks to serve with drinks or as starters to a meal. We serve a mixed plate of crostini which includes our pepper-covered curd cheese, chickpea and garlic purée, anchovy and olive paste, avocado and chilli and other seasonal spreads.

To make the crostini, preheat the oven to 190°C/375°F/Gas Mark 5. Cut small slices of bread from any type of loaf, using a pastry cutter, if you like, place the slices on a baking sheet and drizzle olive oil over them (about 2 tablespoons). Season with a sprinkling of sea salt and freshly ground black pepper and bake for about 10 minutes. Don't put the toppings on too soon or the crostini will lose their crispness.

Above: Anchovy and Olive Tapenade
Opposite: Organic Café Bruschetta

ANCHOVY AND OLIVE PASTE (TAPENADE)

SERVES 6 AS A STARTER

250g (9oz) pitted black olives
55g (2oz) anchovy fillets – do try and use the fresh fillets, sold in brine by good fishmongers
25g (1oz) capers, drained
1½ cloves garlic, peeled
2 tablespoons cold-pressed olive oil
squeeze of lemon juice (optional)
½ teaspoon coarse grain mustard (optional)

Place all the above ingredients in a blender or food processor and blend until smooth and thoroughly mixed. Keep in a covered bowl in the refrigerator for up to 3 months. (Elizabeth David's tapenade contains tuna fish, which gives a much richer and more substantial dish. To make her version, add about 55g [2oz] canned tuna to this recipe.)

STUFFING FOR PRESERVED PEPPERS

You can use this tapenade to stuff preserved peppers. Choose very small peppers, make an incision in the side and extract the seeds before putting the peppers to soak in vinegar for approximately 2 weeks. Then dry them and stuff them with the tapenade mixture (leave out the tuna fish). Arrange in a jar and cover with oil. Taken from Heyraud's *La Cuisine à Nice*.

CHICKPEA AND GARLIC PASTE (HUMMOUS)

SERVES 6

115g (4oz) dried chickpeas
juice of 2 lemons
2 cloves garlic, crushed
4 tablespoons olive oil
1 teaspoon cayenne pepper
sea salt
150ml (¼ pint) tahini

Either soak the chickpeas in a bowl of water overnight or place them in a bowl, cover with boiling water and soak for 2 hours.

Throw the liquid away, then place the chickpeas in a saucepan and cover with fresh water. Cover, bring to the boil and simmer for about 1½-2 hours, until the chickpeas are tender. Drain them and reserve the cooking liquid.

Place the chickpeas in a blender or food processor with the lemon juice, garlic, oil, cayenne pepper, salt and 150ml (¼ pint) of the cooking liquid from the chickpeas. Blend until smooth, then with the motor running, gradually add the tahini until well mixed. If the mixture is too thick, add more cooking liquid and blend to mix – the consistency should be similar to mayonnaise.

Preparation (above) and completion (opposite) of Organic Café Crostini.

AUBERGINE TERRINE

This soft, savoury, layered spread looks beautiful when cut and laid on bruschetta or serve it as you would any other terrine.

SERVES 4-6

900g (2lb) aubergine, cut in half lengthways and baked in the oven at 180°C/350°F/Gas Mark 4 for 45 minutes until soft, then cooled, peeled and chopped

2 teaspoons olive oil

1 clove garlic, crushed

125ml (4fl oz) plain fromage frais

55g (2oz) fresh parmesan cheese, grated

55g (2oz) tasty hard cheese, such as cheddar or Lancashire, grated

3 eggs

6 teaspoons plain flour

sea salt and freshly ground black pepper

2 oven-roasted red peppers, skinned, deseeded and cut into small pieces

4 halves oven-roasted tomatoes

1 handful fresh basil leaves, chopped, plus extra for garnish

Line a 900g (2lb) terrine dish or loaf tin with buttered greaseproof paper and set aside. Preheat the oven to 180°C/350°F/Gas Mark 4. Place the aubergines, oil, garlic, fromage frais, cheeses, eggs, flour and seasoning in a blender or food processor and blend until smooth.

Pour half the aubergine mixture into the prepared terrine dish. Arrange the peppers, tomatoes and chopped basil in layers over the top. Pour the rest of the aubergine mixture on top and level the surface.

Place in a bain marie and bake in the oven for 45-60 minutes until set. Set aside to cool, then cover and chill before serving. Turn out onto a serving plate and serve in slices with a fresh tomato and basil sauce made by blending skinned fresh tomatoes with olive oil, salt and pepper and adding torn basil leaves at the end.

HOMEMADE MAYONNAISE

Of course the most wonderful thing to spread on bread – which we use for all our sandwiches, hot and cold – is the classic mayonnaise. If there is one thing which causes arguments in our kitchens it is how to make mayonnaise. I give you my own version here, which is quick and easy, and, of course, the best!

MAKES 300ml (½ pint)

2 eggs
1 teaspoon mixed sea salt (or Marigold vegetable stock powder) and freshly ground black pepper
1 teaspoon Dijon mustard
100ml (3½fl oz) cold-pressed olive oil
100ml (3½fl oz) cold-pressed sunflower oil
2 tablespoons cider vinegar

Place the eggs together with the salt and pepper (or stock powder) and mustard in a blender or food processor. Start the motor running and combine these ingredients with a short whizz. With the motor running, start adding oil in a thin stream, using the olive oil first, followed by the sunflower oil. When it begins to thicken, add the vinegar. Turn off the motor as soon as the vinegar is incorporated. Use immediately or store in a covered container in the refrigerator for up to 3 days.

You can add most things successfully to mayonnaise! Think of 'Chicken Elizabeth', where curry powder, cream and apricot jam are combined with the mayonnaise and then mixed with the chicken, or the Greek mix of mayonnaise with mashed potatoes to make 'Skordalia'. The following ideas are further variations on this theme.

AIOLI FROM SOUTHERN FRANCE

If you have a problem controlling the size of your girth, this could be your undoing – aioli is addictive! Use it as a dip for raw vegetables or waxy new potatoes cooked in their skins. Mix it into soups (the French call it 'bourride' when mixed into fish soups). Basically, add 3 crushed cloves of garlic per person to your mayonnaise, before you add the oil, and … *voilà*, you have aioli!

ROMESCO FROM CATALUNIA

Blend mayonnaise with tomatoes, sweet red peppers, garlic, ground almonds and half a slice of crumbled bread for another great bread spread that is also wonderful served with cold white fish such as cod or haddock

TONNATO FROM ITALY

This mayonnaise has tuna and anchovies added to it and is the classic accompaniment to the Italian dish, 'Vittello Tonnato'.

SAVOURY BUTTERS

Savoury butters are under-rated as spreads, as accompaniments to boiled or steamed vegetables and jacket potatoes or baked in bread like garlic bread. Try butter mixed with crushed garlic and mashed with capers, or butter mixed with crushed or finely chopped fresh tarragon. *Anchoiade*, the classic provençale butter is made with olive oil – the anchovies and garlic pounded together first – then mixed with the oil and a little vinegar. But beware, anchovies and red wine are an unbeatable combination for bringing on attacks of gout.

Left: Make sure that you buy organic rather than free range eggs (see page 14). Right: Homemade Mayonnaise.

PIZZAS

Legend has it that the original pizza consisted of a base of polenta — which is boiled maize flour — covered with tomato, but the Neapolitans transformed it by using a thin layer of risen bread dough as a base for the tomato sauce.

PIZZA NEAPOLITANA

Make it at home once and you'll never buy it again.

MAKES FOUR 25cm (10in) PIZZAS

FOR THE BASIC PIZZA DOUGH:

25g (1oz) fresh yeast or 15g (½ oz) dried yeast

300ml (½ pint) warm water

½ teaspoon sea salt

2 tablespoons olive oil, plus extra for brushing

600g (1lb 5oz) pasta flour or plain white flour

FOR THE TOMATO SAUCE:

450g (1lb) ripe tomatoes, skinned and chopped or 400g (14oz) can organic chopped tomatoes (don't be tempted to use non-organic tomatoes as you will not achieve the rich tomato taste)

1 clove garlic, crushed

sea salt and freshly ground black pepper

FOR THE TOPPING (per pizza base):

12 anchovies (we use the marinated pink anchovy fillets available from good fishmongers)

1 clove garlic, crushed

12 natural black pitted olives

1 tablespoon grated fresh parmesan cheese

1 teaspoon coarsely ground black pepper

1 tablespoon each of chopped fresh basil and oregano olive oil, for drizzling

Opposite: Pissaladière

First make the dough. Dissolve the fresh yeast in the warm water, then stir in the salt and 2 tablespoons olive oil (if using dried yeast, follow the packet instructions). Place the flour onto a work surface in a heap and make a well in the middle. Pour the yeast liquid into the well and mix into the flour with your hands until it all comes together to make a dough.

Knead for about 10 minutes until smooth and springy. Form into a large ball and place in an oiled bowl. Cover with a warm, damp tea cloth or clingfilm and leave to rise at room temperature for about 1 hour, until the dough has doubled in size.

Meanwhile, make the tomato sauce. Place the tomatoes, garlic and seasoning in a blender or food processor and blend until smooth. Set aside.

Turn the dough out onto a lightly floured surface and knock it back to get rid of the air bubbles, then divide into four balls and press each one out with your hands, starting from the centre and working out, until you have a rough rounded shape about 5mm (¼in) thick.

Preheat the oven to 230°C/450°F/Gas Mark 8. Oil two large baking sheets and place two dough rounds on each baking sheet. Brush the dough with oil and top with the tomato sauce. Onto each base, place the topping ingredients in the order that they are listed.

Drizzle some oil over the surface and bake in the oven for about 10 minutes. The pizzas are ready when the bottom is very crisp and brown and the top has melted into a delicious bubbling mass.

PISSALADIERE

MAKES 6 LARGE PORTIONS

Preheat the oven to 180°C/350°F/Gas Mark 4. Using the same recipe for the basic pizza dough (see Pizza Neapolitana recipe), oil a rectangular 30 x 15cm (12 x 6in) baking tin and press the dough into it with your fingers. Cover with a warm, damp tea cloth and set aside for about 20 minutes. Meanwhile, prepare the following ingredients for the topping.

6 tablespoons olive oil

1.3kg (3lb) onions, sliced

2 cloves garlic, crushed

sea salt and freshly ground black pepper

115g (4oz) fresh or canned anchovies

12 natural black pitted olives

chopped fresh thyme, rosemary and sage,
   for sprinkling

Heat the oil in a large saucepan and fry
the onions until they are soft and brown,
stirring occasionally, then add the garlic, and
salt and pepper to taste. Spread this mixture
onto the dough and top with the anchovies
and black olives. Sprinkle the herbs over
the top. Bake in the oven for 30 minutes,
then cut into squares and serve with a
green salad.

ORGANIC CAFE PIZZA

Make the pizzas as before (following the basic
pizza dough recipe for Pizza Neapolitana) but
instead of using the anchovy topping, finish with
the following ingredients in the order in which
they are listed.

PER PIZZA BASE:

175g (6oz) soft curd cheese
   (see recipe on page 152 for home-made
   curd cheese)

115g (4oz) onions, sliced and caramelized
   in olive oil

115g (4oz) mushrooms, sliced

25g (1oz) pine nuts, lightly oven-toasted

freshly grated parmesan cheese, to sprinkle

chopped fresh thyme and rosemary,
   to sprinkle

sea salt and freshly ground black pepper

Mainstays of the store cupboard, flour, eggs and olive oil provide the wonderfully simple basis of pasta, one of the most versatile foods there is.

PASTAS

We do not make all our own pasta as good quality dry organic pasta is hard to beat. But we generally make our own ravioli, tagliatelle, fettucine and lasagne. The basic difference between these three is in the width of the pasta. The width of fettucine is 3mm (⅛in), the width of tagliatelle is 5mm (¼in) and the width of lasagne is 4cm (2¼in).

Once you have the thin sheets of pasta rolled out, all that remains is to decide on fettucine (3mm/⅛ in thick), tagliatelle (5mm/¼ in thick) or lasagne (4cm/2¼in thick).

FRESH PASTA DOUGH

SERVES 4

225g (8oz) plain white flour or pasta flour
1 teaspoon salt
2 eggs
1 egg white
1 tablespoon olive oil

Place the flour and salt in a mound on a work surface and press a hole in the centre. Drop the eggs, egg white and oil into the hole and whisk them around with your fingertips in a continuous circular movement, introducing more flour as you go. Work in sufficient flour to produce a firm and elastic dough. It must be dry enough not to stick to your fingers or the work surface, if not, work in more flour.

Divide the dough into 4 pieces and roll each out until about 1cm (½in) thick. Introduce each piece of dough into the pasta machine, guiding the paste through the machine with your hands to form 4 thin sheets of dough. If rolling out by hand, allow yourself a large area of work surface and roll out the paste with an even pressure away from you into a long oblong. The dough must be thin and even, thinner than a penny (approximately 2mm/1⁄16in thick).

Leave the sheets of paste for a bit so that the egg dries a little, then take a pastry cutter or sharp knife and divide it into long thin ribbons of the required width, depending on which pasta you are making. This needs a steady hand and eye, as long even strands are the goal! Hang up to dry before use. Cook the pasta in a large saucepan of fast boiling, salted water for 7 minutes, drain and serve.

RAVIOLI

Use the basic pasta dough as above to make ravioli for about 6 people. This makes thirty-six 6cm (2½in) squares or seventy-two 4cm (1½in) smaller squares.

Prepare the basic pasta dough as above, then divide it in half and roll out each half into a thin paste, about 2mm (1⁄16in) thick, but not too thin as it will tear. To make square ravioli, mark one sheet of paste into squares using a sharp knife (it is easier if you use a ruler!). Place the stuffing or filling in the centre of each square on the sheet of pasta, then with a brush, wet the lines across and down between the stuffing and lay the second sheet of paste gently on the top. Press down the lines both ways between the stuffing until the paste sticks together. Separate the squares with a sharp knife or pastry cutter and, if necessary, stick the edges together again by applying water with your fingers and pressing together.

An alternative way to achieve the half-moon pouches is to use a 5cm (2in) pastry cutter and

To make the round ravioli pictured here, place a spoonful of stuffing at regular intervals on the sheet of pasta. Using a pastry brush, wet the pasta in a circle following the edge of a 5cm/2in pastry cutter. Lay a second sheet of pasta on top and using the pastry cutter, cut around each round of stuffing. Seal with your fingers to finish.

cut out a series of circles. Fill the centres of the circles with your stuffing, wet the edges and fold over in a half circle pressing the edges together to make little stuffed half-moons.

Cook the ravioli in a large saucepan of fast boiling, salted water for about 7 minutes, drain and serve.

PUMPKIN RAVIOLI WITH GINGER SAUCE

These delicately flavoured ravioli surrounded by a light consommé-style sauce look very pretty.

SERVES 6
FOR THE FILLING:
   1 small pumpkin (roasted, peeled, deseeded and mashed)
   2 tablespoons grated fresh parmesan cheese
   55g (2oz) creme fraiche
   ½ beaten egg
   1 dessertspoon fresh parsley, chopped
   sea salt and freshly ground black pepper

Mix together the ingredients and use to fill the ravioli pouches (see page 38). Cook the pumpkin ravioli in a large saucepan of fast boiling, salted water for about 7 minutes, then drain and serve with the ginger sauce.

FOR THE SAUCE:
   55g (2oz) fresh root ginger, peeled and cut into 2.5cm (1in) sticks
   150ml (¼ pint) white wine
   300ml (½ pint) vegetable stock
   juice of 1 lemon

Place the ginger, wine and stock in a saucepan, bring to the boil and boil rapidly, uncovered. Stir in the lemon juice, then return to the boil and boil rapidly to reduce further, until thick, stirring occasionally. Serve in a large open soup bowl with the cooked pumpkin ravioli placed in the middle.

CURD CHEESE AND PINE NUT RAVIOLI

SERVES 6
   115g (4oz) curd cheese (see recipe on page 152)
   1 tablespoon chopped mixed fresh herbs, such as basil, oregano and thyme
   sea salt and freshly ground black pepper
   1 tablespoon pine nuts, oven-roasted until golden

In a bowl, mash the curd cheese together with the herbs and seasoning, then add the pine nuts and mix well. Divide the mixture amongst the ravioli pouches (see page 38). Cook the ravioli in a large saucepan of fast boiling, salted water for about 7 minutes, then drain and serve with basic tomato sauce (see following recipe).

BASIC TOMATO SAUCE

SERVES 4 (generous portions)
   2 tablespoons olive oil
   1 onion, chopped
   1 carrot, diced
   1 stick celery, chopped
   2 cloves garlic, crushed
   1 bay leaf
   sea salt and freshly ground black pepper
   450g (1lb) fresh tomatoes, skinned, deseeded and chopped or 400g (14oz) can chopped tomatoes
   1 tablespoon brown sugar

Heat the oil in a pan, add the onion, carrot, celery and garlic and cook for a few minutes, until softened, stirring occasionally. Add the bay leaf and seasoning, then the tomatoes and sugar. Bring to the boil, then reduce the heat, cover and simmer for 30 minutes, stirring once or twice. Discard the bay leaf, and purée the sauce in a blender until smooth. Reheat and serve with torn basil leaves.

Opposite: Pumpkin Ravioli with Ginger Sauce

NOUILLES

This French version of an Italian ribbon pasta differs only because of the greater number of egg yolks used in proportion to the flour, but I find that it is more satisfying than Italian pasta when eaten as an accompaniment, tossed in butter or olive oil.

SERVES 4
    280g (10oz) plain white flour or pasta flour
    pinch of sea salt
    1 whole egg
    6 egg yolks

Place the flour in a mound on a board or work surface. Make a hole in the middle and put the salt in it. Beat the whole egg with the egg yolks and pour this into the hole in the flour. With the tips of your fingers, work the flour into the eggs until it is all a lively springy mass – take the flour into the eggs from the sides of the hole little by little until well mixed together. Place in a bowl, cover and leave in a cool place for about 1 hour.

Divide the dough in half and roll out each half to a thickness of about 2mm (⅟₁₆in) and cut into strips 5mm (¼in) in diameter. Cook in a large saucepan of salted, boiling water for about 5 minutes. Drain and serve as an accompaniment to meat and vegetable dishes, or as a dish in its own right with a quick sauce or simply butter and freshly grated parmesan cheese.

You can also cook these noodles in the oven in a similar way to macaroni cheese – perhaps with a topping of ham, parmesan cheese and cream.

QUICK PASTA SAUCES

SPICY CLAM SAUCE
SERVES 4
    2 cloves garlic
    1-2 small red chillies, deseeded and finely chopped
        (number depends on how hot you want the sauce)

2 tablespoons olive oil
300ml (½ pint) dry white wine
1 quantity basic tomato sauce (see recipe on page 40)
large handful of fresh parsley, finely chopped
sea salt and freshly ground black pepper
450g (1lb) pasta, such as spaghetti or fettucine
450g (1lb) live clams, scrubbed

Fry the garlic and chilli gently in the olive oil until soft, stirring occasionally. Pour in the wine and let it bubble until the liquid is reduced by half. Add the tomato sauce, parsley and seasoning. Bring to the boil again, cover and simmer for 20 minutes, stirring occasionally. Bring a large pan of salted water to the boil and cook the pasta according to packet instructions – I prefer thin pasta with this, either packet spaghetti or fettucine – check to make sure you remove it from the water while still firm to the bite.

Meanwhile cook the clams. Discard any clams that don't close when sharply tapped, then tip them into a large pan over a high heat and cover. Steam for a couple of minutes in their own liquid. Throw away any clams that have not opened, then add the rest to the tomato sauce and leave to simmer while you drain the pasta. Place the pasta in a large serving bowl, add the clams and tomato sauce and toss to mix.

BROCCOLI, ANCHOVY AND FETA CHEESE SAUCE
This recipe was suggested by the editor of this book Anna Mumford and it is really delicious and unusual.

SERVES 4 (WITH 450g [1lb] OF PASTA)
    500g (1lb 2oz) broccoli
    2 cloves garlic, chopped
    2 tablespoons olive oil
    50g (1¾oz) can anchovies, drained and chopped
    200g (7oz) feta cheese, cut into small chunks
    sea salt and freshly ground black pepper

Opposite: Tagliatelle with Basic Tomato Sauce

Break the broccoli into small florets and boil quickly or steam over a pan of boiling water until just tender, then drain. Sauté the garlic in the oil until soft, then add the anchovies, steamed broccoli and feta. Add to the cooked pasta, toss to mix, season and serve.

RICOTTA (OR CREAM CHEESE), CAPERS AND BLACK OLIVE SAUCE

SERVES 4 (WITH 450g [1lb] PASTA)

Simply stir 2 tablespoons olive oil, 115g (4oz) ricotta cheese, 115g (4oz) black olives and 55g (2oz) chopped capers into the cooked and drained pasta. Season with salt and plenty of freshly ground black pepper. Top with chopped fresh parsley if you have it to hand and serve.

WALNUT PESTO

SERVES 4 (WITH 450g [1lb] PASTA)

    175g (6oz) walnuts, shelled
    1 clove garlic
    1 tablespoon pine nuts
    50g (1¾oz) butter
    ½ tablespoon olive oil
    50g (1¾oz) fresh basil leaves, plus extra for garnish
    100g (3½oz) parmesan cheese, freshly grated
    sea salt and freshly ground black pepper

Plunge the walnuts and garlic into boiling water to loosen their skins, reserving about 10 walnuts for garnishing. Pop the walnuts out of their skins and grind them together with the pine nuts in a food processor. Melt the butter in a heavy-based pan and gently sauté the nuts for 5 minutes, stirring occasionally. Return the nuts to the processor together with the peeled garlic, olive oil, basil leaves, parmesan and seasoning.

   Liquidize quickly until all the ingredients are amalgamated. The consistency should be one of a traditional pesto sauce. Mix thoroughly with the cooked pasta and garnish with the reserved walnuts (chopped), and basil leaves.

Opposite: Vegetarian Lasagne

VEGETARIAN LASAGNE

A great standby for family gatherings, the 'meatless mince' lasagne is popular with everyone.

SERVES 4

You can use dried lasagne sheets but if you want to make your own pasta, follow the recipe on page 37 until the point at which you have long oblongs of pasta 2mm (¹⁄₁₆in) thick. Cut into rectangles 10 x 5cm (4 x 2in). In a large saucepan bring 3 litres (5¼ pints) salted water to the boil adding a few drops of olive oil. Cook the strips of pasta, a few at a time, until they float to the surface. Remove and drain well, then lay them on a damp cloth. Use as required.

   Preheat the oven to 180°C/350°F/Gas Mark 4. Make the meatless mince (see page 50) and then the béchamel sauce (see recipe below). Layer the lasagne sheets with the meatless mince and béchamel sauce. Start by ladling half of the béchamel sauce over the bottom of a greased oven-proof lasagne dish, then lay one sheet of lasagne, one layer of meatless mince, then lasagne, then mince, then lasagne, finishing off with the remaining béchamel sauce to cover the pasta completely and a generous sprinkling of freshly grated parmesan cheese on top. Bake in the oven for about 30 minutes until browned and bubbling.

BECHAMEL SAUCE

MAKES 600ml (1 pint)

    55g (2oz) butter
    4 tablespoons plain flour
    600ml (1 pint) milk
    sea salt and freshly ground black pepper

Place the butter in a small, heavy-based saucepan and melt over a gentle heat. Add the flour and blend into the melted butter to make a smooth ball or *roux*, stirring continuously for about 2 minutes, before gradually adding the milk. Continue stirring and bring to the boil. Simmer gently for 1-2 minutes, stirring, then season with salt and pepper.

Four seasons of vegetables

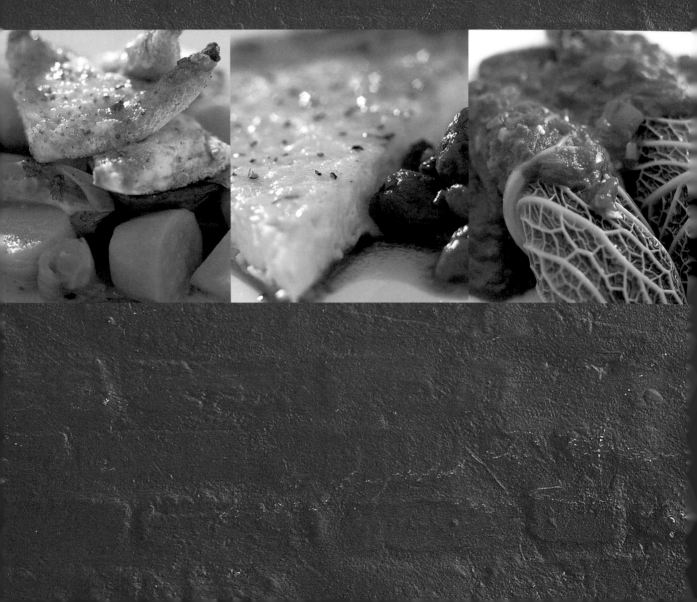

When you cook with organic vegetables allow yourself to be lead by the produce which, of course, changes from season to season. Far from being restrictive, this discipline adds variety to the daily repertoire of dishes and each season sparks off favourites which can be repeated from year to year. Winter is a quiet period, when fresh ingredients are often expensive and less readily available — so it is a good time to use dried beans, dried fruits and preserves. Spring brings young shoots and tender vegetables like asparagus and peas. Summer heralds the start of the main salad and vegetable season as well as soft fruit and wonderful berries followed by autumn's rich harvest of squash and root vegetables.

The growing of vegetables on conventional farms today is a pitiful practice and the use of pesticides is, to my mind, pure lunacy. If you could look at a farm before the last war, you would see how fundamental the change has been. In those days, farms were self-sufficient units following seasonal cycles and living in a symbiotic relationship with their environment. Nowadays, farming is seen as an industry – not a way of life. Large-scale farming, with its use of sophisticated machinery, chemical pesticides and fertilizers, hits the environment hard, while nobody knows the extent of the damage done by pesticide residues in our food, which amounts to a cocktail sprayed every year estimated to be in the region of 450g (1lb) per person. Common daily food, such as apples and lettuces are regularly sprayed with more than 20 different pesticides during their short lives. And no, it doesn't all wash off …

BART IVES AND SPITALFIELDS

Bart Ives grows all the vegetables he sells at London's Spitalfields Organic Market on his own smallholding. Every year we eagerly await his wild salad leaves which he begins to pick in March. Many of these you will find as weeds in your own garden or even in your window boxes! There is dandelion, rocket, mizuna, red mint and pak choi. Add a little baby spinach to this mix and you have a wonderful, peppery, rich-tasting salad.

Sunday morning shopping at Spitalfields Organic Market in London.

RIVERFORD FARM

From a farm of just 3 acres in 1986, Guy Watson of Riverford Farm in South Devon has developed the organization into a 400-acre concern, with up to 60 staff growing, picking, packing and distributing organic vegetables. Not only do they supply multiples, wholesalers and local shops, but they have a very successful 'box scheme' supplying organic vegetables to over 2,000 households in Devon, Cornwall, Somerset, Dorset, Gloucestershire, London, Watford and Kent.

How were they able to achieve this phenomenal success? Amazingly, there were still enough people farming traditional mixed farms in South Devon to get together with Guy to form an organic farmers' group. The group is run as a co-operative and going from strength to strength with some new members intending to offer organic lamb, beef, cheese and even wine as well as vegetables.

The South Devon Organic Producers' Co-operative has clearly defined aims, and, since these coincide with our own, we are delighted to do business with them. They aim to produce and sell high quality organic vegetables in a way that is affordable to all – something which is vital if the market for organic foods is to grow. They are also committed to providing long-term security for the small and medium farms which make up its members. Finally, they are supplying food from a known source – food that is grown in a way which causes the least impact on the environment and the most benefit to the local community – a priority that is most important to us with our commitment to tracing the source of all our food.

Gathering leeks for organic vegetable boxes in February at Riverford Farm, South Devon.

SPRING

The first hint of spring reminds me of 'Gyp Pot' an invention of my sister Sally. During the Easter holidays from school, we would build a fire at the bottom of the garden, root up and pick all the newly sprouting vegetables and cook the results in a battered old saucepan. We called this smoky earthy concoction 'Gyp Pot', fondly imagining that this is what the gypsies did.

CARROT AND GINGER SOUP

This is a good soup to start the spring. It puts the zip back into sluggish winter blood.

SERVES 4
   900g (2lb) carrots, chopped
   850ml (1½ pints) vegetable stock
   4 tablespoons butter
   1 onion, chopped
   1 clove garlic, crushed
   25g (1oz) fresh root ginger, peeled and finely chopped
   sea salt and freshly ground black pepper
   850ml (1½ pints) double cream or Greek yoghurt
      (optional)

Place the carrots and stock in a large pan. Bring to the boil, then cover, reduce the heat and simmer for 15 minutes, stirring occasionally. Meanwhile, melt the butter in a separate pan, add the onion, garlic and ginger and sauté until soft and browning, stirring occasionally.

Cool the carrot mixture slightly, then place in a blender or food processor with the onion mixture and blend until smooth. Return to the rinsed-out pan, add seasoning to taste and reheat gently before serving.

If you are adding the cream or yoghurt, whisk it into the soup and heat for a further minute. For a more sophisticated starter, add a dash of sherry just before serving, swirl a little of the cream or yoghurt on top and finish with a sprinkling of finely chopped fresh parsley.

SHEPHERDESS PIE WITH MEATLESS MINCE

Lizzie, our head chef at the cookshop, came up with this when we wanted to make vegetarian shepherd's pie. We also use the mince for veggie bolognese, cannelloni and lasagne.

SERVES 4
FOR THE MEATLESS MINCE:
   1 large onion, chopped
   2 tablespoons olive oil
   1 clove garlic, crushed
   115g (4oz) carrot, diced
   2 sticks celery, chopped
   225g (8oz) whole green lentils cooked in plenty of
      boiling water for 45-50 minutes until tender
      or two 400g (14oz) cans lentils
   225g (8oz) can chopped tomatoes
   2 tablespoons tomato purée
   2 tablespoons chopped fresh parsley
   sea salt and freshly ground black pepper or stock
      powder, for seasoning
FOR THE PIE TOPPING:
   700g (1lb 9oz) mashed potatoes
   25g (1oz) butter
   sea salt and freshly ground black pepper

Preheat the oven to 190°C/375°F/Gas Mark 5. To make the meatless mince, fry the onion in the oil until soft and brown, stirring occasionally, then add the garlic, carrot and celery. Cover the pan and cook gently for about 15

Opposite: Carrot and Ginger Soup

minutes until tender.

Drain the lentils, reserving a little of the cooking liquid. Stir the lentils into the onion mixture with the tomatoes, tomato purée, parsley and a little of the reserved lentil liquid seasoned with salt and pepper or stock powder. The sauce should be a thick, moist consistency.

Place the meatless mince in a suitable ovenproof dish. Prepare the pie topping by mixing the mashed potatoes, butter and seasoning together and spreading it on top of the mince to cover it completely. Cook in the oven for about 20 minutes or until golden brown.

LUSTY OMELETTE OF SPRING VEGETABLES

Frittata, omelette and tortilla are all versions of the same thing, that is, vegetables mixed into whisked eggs and cooked!

You can cook them on the hob but I prefer the oven-baked version for a more substantial meal.

You can put anything you fancy in these thick, lusty omelettes. So, although this is a spring version, it can easily be adapted to take tomatoes and cheese, carrots and sweet potatoes – anything. Well, almost anything! Here I use fresh peas, asparagus, little courgettes, all finely chopped, and the all-important new potatoes.

SERVES 4

4 large new potatoes, scrubbed and diced

450g (1lb) prepared mixed spring vegetables, finely chopped

2 tablespoons olive oil

25g (1oz) butter

2 onions, thinly sliced

2 cloves garlic, crushed

8 eggs

1 tablespoon chopped fresh parsley

1 teaspoon chopped fresh thyme

sea salt and freshly ground black pepper

25g (1oz) freshly grated parmesan cheese (optional)

Lightly pre-cook the vegetables in a saucepan of fast boiling, lightly salted water, starting with the potatoes and cooking them for about 10 minutes, then adding the rest of the spring vegetables and cooking for a further 5 minutes or so. When the potatoes are soft but firm and the rest of the vegetables are *al dente*, drain and set aside.

Heat 1 tablespoon oil with the butter in a 20cm (8in) frying pan and fry the onions gently for about 25 minutes, or until golden brown, stirring occasionally. Stir in the garlic.

While the onions are cooking, whisk the eggs in a large bowl, add the parsley and thyme and season with salt and pepper. Remove the onions and garlic from the pan and add to the egg mixture. Add the other pre-cooked vegetables and fold into the egg mixture, together with the parmesan cheese, if using.

Preheat the oven to 180°C/350°F/Gas Mark 4. Heat the remaining oil in a 20cm (8in) heavy-based, ovenproof pan. Run the oil evenly around the sides of the pan, pour in the egg mixture and cook on the hob over a low heat for 5 minutes, then transfer to the oven. Cook for a further 10 minutes or until firm. Ease from the sides of the pan using a spatula and serve in slices or wedges. Serve on its own or with a salsa (see page 156).

Opposite: Lusty Omelette of Spring Vegetables

STIR-FRIED VEGETABLES WITH CASHEW NUTS AND BROWN RICE

Agatha and Walter Schwager are true cosmopolitans – Dutch and Indonesian by birth they now live in the Chinese quarter of Toronto in Canada. When we visit we spend hours in the local stores marvelling at the exotic mushrooms, and unidentifiable green shoots and leaves which we take home and make into a version of this stir-fry. This recipe can be adapted to work with virtually anything you have delivered in your weekly vegetable box.

SERVES 4

225g (8oz) short grain brown rice
1 teaspoon salt
2 tablespoons sesame oil
1 teaspoon grated fresh root ginger
2 cloves garlic, crushed
115g (4oz) cashew nuts
2 leeks, washed and cut into matchsticks
2 carrots, cut into matchsticks
½ cabbage, finely shredded
115g (4oz) mushrooms, chopped
2 tablespoons tamari
sea salt and freshly ground black pepper

Put the rice in a large saucepan with the teaspoon of salt and 700ml (1¼ pints) water. Do not cover, but bring to the boil first and then cover with a tightly fitting lid. Simmer for about 40 minutes or until the water has been absorbed and the rice is tender.

In a wok, heat the sesame oil and add the ginger, garlic and cashew nuts. Stir-fry them quickly over a high heat for about 3 minutes, before adding all the prepared vegetables and the tamari. Stir-fry for a further 5 minutes – the vegetables should be crunchy. Then add the cooked rice to the mixture in the wok. Stir-fry together with a tossing movement for a further 3 minutes or until the rice is hot. Adjust the seasoning and serve. If you like spicy food, try a little chilli jam on the side (see page 154).

SUMMER RECIPES

Summer for me would not be complete without a cold Vichyssoise soup made from potatoes and leeks and swirled with thick cream. But I have, in the end, given this space to a more original and certainly more healthy soup option – I have also kept a friend into the bargain!

GARLIC AND POTATO SOUP

Friends' recipes, of course, must be part of every cook's repertoire. This one was cooked for us by Marina Martin when she had the inspired idea of inviting her close circle of female friends to a Tuscan farmhouse one summer. She is a theatre agent and the group was colourful and interesting. We sunned ourselves around a pool set in the middle of an olive grove and in the evenings wrote a risqué novel together on my laptop – often while eating this soup!

Opposite:
Char-grilled, Marinated Tofu served with Stir-fried Vegetables and Brown Rice (see page 60).

SERVES 4

3 heads garlic

900g (2lb) potatoes, peeled and diced

1.2 litres (2 pints) vegetable stock

sea salt and freshly ground black pepper

cold-pressed olive oil, to drizzle

2 tablespoons mixed chopped fresh parsley and chives

Separate the cloves of garlic and place them in boiling water for 30 seconds then drain. This enables you to pop the cloves out of their skins more easily, but also makes the garlic taste sweeter which is important for this soup. Place the garlic and potatoes in a pan with the vegetable stock and bring to the boil. Cover, reduce the heat and simmer until the potatoes are soft, stirring occasionally.

Remove the pan from the heat and remove and discard the garlic cloves. Allow the soup to cool slightly then purée in a blender or food processor until smooth. Return to the saucepan, add salt and pepper to taste, then reheat gently before serving. Ladle into soup bowls and drizzle a little olive oil over the top of the soup, sprinkling the herbs over the oil. You can also serve this soup cold with a swirl of cream instead of oil.

CAESAR SALAD

This classic recipe comes from our head chef Issa Cissockla.

SERVES 4

FOR THE SALAD:

1 head cos lettuce

2 heads baby gem lettuce

1 large slice focaccia, or other bread, cut into cubes

2 tablespoons extra virgin olive oil

4 tablespoons freshly grated parmesan cheese, plus shavings to serve

16 fresh anchovy fillets (optional)

sea salt and freshly ground black pepper

FOR THE DRESSING:

1 tablespoon lemon juice

2 cloves garlic, crushed

1 tablespoon Worcestershire sauce

½ tablespoon horseradish sauce

1 tablespoon balsamic vinegar

1 egg

125ml (4fl oz) rapeseed oil

125ml (4fl oz) extra virgin olive oil

To make the salad, first separate the lettuce leaves discarding any damaged ones. Rinse, drain and pat dry. Wrap them in a clean tea towel and chill until ready to serve.

Preheat the oven to 190°C/375°F/Gas Mark 5. Toss the cubes of bread with the olive oil in a bowl, then spread them out in a single layer on a baking sheet. Sprinkle with the parmesan and a pinch of salt. Bake in the oven for 5 minutes until crisp and golden. Drain off any excess fat on absorbent kitchen paper or a clean, dry cloth and set aside.

To make the dressing, combine the lemon juice, garlic, Worcestershire sauce, horseradish sauce and balsamic vinegar in a mixing bowl. Set aside. Cook the egg in boiling water, in its shell, for about 3 minutes, then scoop out the runny yolk and white and add to the dressing. Whisk together with an electric mixer. Add the rapeseed oil a tablespoon at a time, whisking continuously, then whisk in the olive oil and season to taste with salt and pepper.

Place the lettuce leaves in a salad bowl. Pour over the dressing to taste and toss to coat. Sprinkle over the parmesan croutons and scatter with parmesan shavings and optional anchovy fillets. Serve immediately. Store any leftover dressing, covered, in the refrigerator for up to 2 days.

AUBERGINES IMAM BAYELDI

This is another excellent summer dish which, by all accounts, was named after an over-indulgent rich Turk called Bayeldi! I like to serve it as a starter, but it can also be a main dish. Serve with warm bread. Our Yoghurt and Herb Bread makes a perfect combination (see page 26).

Opposite: Caesar Salad, with fresh anchovy fillets.

SERVES 4

4 aubergines

sea salt and freshly ground black pepper

2 tablespoons olive oil, plus extra for pouring

4 onions, finely chopped

4 tomatoes, skinned and chopped

½ teaspoon ground allspice

1 tablespoon chopped fresh parsley

55g (2oz) currants or raisins

1 clove garlic, peeled

1 bay leaf

Remove the stalks from the aubergines and make several incisions from top to bottom on each aubergine, taking care not to cut right the way through. Place them in a colander and sprinkle with salt (see caption below) and set aside to drain for about 1 hour.

Heat 2 tablespoons oil in a pan, add the onions and cook until they start to brown, stirring occasionally. Stir in the tomatoes, allspice, parsley and seasoning and cook gently for about 5 minutes or until the onions and tomatoes are thoroughly mixed together, stirring occasionally. Add the currants or raisins and cook for a further 2-3 minutes, stirring. Remove from the heat and set aside to cool a little while you rinse and dry the aubergines.

Using a teaspoon, stuff the onion mixture into the aubergines and place them in a flameproof, ovenproof dish, so that they are tight up against each other. Pour in enough olive oil to come half way up the sides of the aubergines. Add the garlic and bay leaf, cover and cook on top of the stove or in a preheated oven at 180°C/350°F/Gas Mark 4 for about 1 hour, or until they are soft. Discard the garlic and bay leaf. Leave the aubergines to cool and serve cold the next day with most of the oil poured off (but not thrown away!).

The oil left from the Imam Bayeldi could be used to make the Roast Vegetable Salad (see page 60).

MELANZANA

Melanzana is Italian for aubergine or to give it its correct English name, egg plant. This simple dish combines ripe tomatoes, herbs, buffalo mozzarella and melanzana.

SERVES 4

1 tablespoon olive oil, plus extra for brushing and sprinkling

½ large onion, finely chopped

3 cloves garlic, crushed

450g (1lb) fresh ripe tomatoes, skinned, deseeded and chopped, or 400g (14oz) can chopped tomatoes

a sprig of fresh thyme, finely chopped

a sprig of fresh rosemary, finely chopped

sea salt and freshly ground black pepper

2 medium-sized aubergines

8 slices buffalo mozzarella cheese

4 tomatoes, sliced

freshly grated parmesan cheese, for sprinkling

Left: To make aubergines less bitter, place them cut in a colander, sprinkle with salt and cover with a weighted plate. Leave to drain for an hour or two.
Opposite: Melanzana

Preheat the oven to 200°C/400°F/Gas Mark 6. Make the tomato sauce. Heat 1 tablespoon oil in a pan and fry the onion and garlic for 5 minutes, stirring occasionally. Add the tomatoes and their juice, herbs and seasoning, bring to the boil, then reduce the heat and cook, uncovered, for about 20 minutes, stirring occasionally. You can either purée the tomato sauce or leave it as a chunky country sauce.

Meanwhile, cut the aubergines into thin slices and brush all over with some oil. Heat a chargrill (if you do not have one of these handy things which, is in fact a ribbed grill pan, you can use a frying pan). Grill the aubergines quickly on either side until nicely browned.

Now layer the aubergines either into individual terracotta dishes or into a greased baking tin. Drizzle a little oil over the bottom of the dish(es), then spoon one-third of the tomato sauce over the oil. Place half the aubergines on the tomato sauce, top with half the mozzarella slices and top this with a slice of tomato. Top again with a layer of the remaining aubergines, tomato, then mozzarella and finally the rest of the tomato sauce. Sprinkle with some grated parmesan cheese.

Bake in the oven for about 15 minutes until cooked through and the mozzarella and tomatoes are bubbling. Serve immediately with crusty country bread and a mixed leaf salad.

ROAST VEGETABLE SALAD

SERVES 4

FOR THE SALAD:
    4 red onions, peeled and quartered
    900g (2lb) small firm potatoes, scrubbed
    900g (2lb) pumpkin, deseeded and sliced into crescents
    8 raw baby beetroot, scrubbed and trimmed
    3 tablespoons olive oil
    2 tablespoons lemon juice
    2 tablespoons chopped fresh oregano
    1 tablespoon chopped fresh thyme
    1 tablespoon coarse sea salt

FOR THE DRESSING:
    3 tablespoons olive oil
    4 tablespoons cider vinegar
    2 tablespoons coarse grain mustard
    cracked peppercorns and parmesan shavings, to garnish

Preheat the oven to 200°C/400°F/Gas Mark 6. Place the onions and potatoes together with the pumpkin and beetroot in a large baking dish.

Pour over the oil and lemon juice, together with the herbs and salt and toss to coat. Bake in the oven for about 45 minutes or until the vegetables are soft.

Remove from the oven and set aside to cool to room temperature. Meanwhile, make the dressing by whisking the olive oil, vinegar and mustard together until thoroughly mixed. Pour the dressing over the vegetables and top with a sprinkling of cracked peppercorns and the parmesan shavings.

CHAR-GRILLED MARINADED TOFU

This is my favourite way to cook tofu, because it absorbs the tastes so well and the texture remains firm, rather like tuna.

SERVES 2 AS A LIGHT LUNCH OR 4 AS A STARTER
    450g (1lb) tofu, cut into 8 fillets, each 1cm (½in) thick
    5 tablespoons tamari (this is naturally fermented soya)
    juice of 2 limes (if you have no limes, lemon juice will do)
    2 teaspoons chopped fresh root ginger
    1 tablespoon chopped fresh coriander
    olive oil, for brushing

Place the tofu in a shallow non-metallic dish. In a small bowl, mix together the tamari, lime juice, ginger and coriander and pour over the tofu, turning the tofu over in the marinade to coat it all over. Cover and leave to marinate in the refrigerator overnight or for at least 4 hours.

Opposite: Tofu marinade of tamari, lime, ginger and coriander.

Heat a griddle pan on top of the stove and brush with oil. Remember that tofu does not have natural oil of its own, so keep the griddle greased or the tofu will taste too charred. Remove the tofu from the marinade and reserve the marinade. Char-grill the tofu fillets for about 2 minutes on each side, until cooked.

Serve on a bed of stir-fried vegetables and rice. To prepare stir-fried vegetables, cut carrots, leeks and courgettes into strips of about 1cm (½in) (or put them through the food processor) and pre-cook some brown rice. Heat 2 tablespoons of cold-pressed sesame oil or olive oil in a wok. Add 1 chopped clove of garlic and 1 teaspoon minced or finely chopped fresh root ginger. Throw in the vegetables with the reserved tofu marinade, 1 tablespoon tamari and salt and pepper, then add the rice. Stir fry together for a few minutes and top with the char-grilled tofu.

COURGETTE AND DILL SOUFFLE

If you are short of time and need to prepare these in advance, you can store them in the fridge for up to 24 hours and reheat them when required.

SERVES 4

40g (1½oz) butter, plus extra for greasing
mixture of breadcrumbs and freshly grated parmesan
    cheese, for coating (optional)
450g (1lb) courgettes, grated
225ml (8fl oz) milk
¼ onion
a pinch of grated nutmeg
a pinch of black peppercorns
40g (1½oz) plain flour
sea salt and freshly ground black pepper
2 eggs, separated, plus one extra egg white
125ml (4fl oz) double cream, plus 4 teaspoons
a handful of fresh dill, finely chopped, plus extra for serving

Opposite: Courgette and Dill Soufflé

Grease four 8 x 8cm (3¼ x 3¼ in) ramekin dishes with a little butter and coat with a mixture of breadcrumbs and parmesan, if liked. Set aside. Preheat the oven to 180°C/350°F/Gas Mark 4. Place the grated courgettes on absorbent kitchen paper and set aside to drain. Place the milk in a saucepan with the onion, nutmeg and peppercorns and heat gently until simmering, then remove the pan from the heat, strain the milk into a bowl and discard the rest.

Melt 40g (1½oz) butter in a clean saucepan, then stir in the flour for about 3 minutes until combined to give a pale yellow paste. Gradually add the strained milk, cooking over a medium heat and whisking constantly for about 3 minutes, until smooth and thick. Add the salt and pepper and remove from the heat. Cool slightly.

Beat together the egg yolks and cream in a bowl, then beat them into the sauce. Stir in the grated courgettes and chopped dill. In a separate bowl, whisk the egg whites until stiff, then fold them into the courgette mixture, using a large metal spoon which allows a better crisp cutting movement than a wooden spoon.

Divide the mixture equally between the prepared ramekins and place in a roasting tin. Pour a little boiling water into the tin around the base of the dishes to create a bain marie and cook in the oven for about 20 minutes. Remove from the oven and allow to cool. When almost

cold, carefully remove the soufflés from the ramekins and keep to one side on a lightly greased dish until needed or in the fridge overnight covered with cling film (they can be kept in the fridge for up to 24 hours).

To serve, preheat the oven to 180°C/350°F/Gas Mark 4 and cook the soufflés for a further 30 minutes. Just before serving, break the soufflés open, drizzle 1 teaspoon cream into each one and sprinkle with a little chopped dill.

GOAT'S CHEESE SOUFFLE

Prepare exactly as above, adding 115g (4oz) crumbled goat's cheese instead of the courgettes and 1 tomato, skinned, deseeded and finely chopped to the mixture. Spoon a little cream – into which you have ground some sea salt and pepper – over the cooked soufflés before serving, if you like.

GOAT'S CHEESE AND PARMESAN TART

SERVES 4

FOR THE PASTRY:

85g (3oz) butter

175g (6oz) plain flour

pinch of salt

1 egg

½ tablespoon milk

FOR THE FILLING:

2 large eggs

225ml (8fl oz) single cream

sea salt and freshly ground black pepper

225g (8oz) soft goat's cheese

115g (4oz) fresh parmesan cheese, grated

Preheat the oven to 180°C/350°F/Gas Mark 4. Make the pastry. In a bowl, rub the butter into the flour and salt until it resembles fine breadcrumbs. Beat the egg and milk together and add to the flour, mixing to form a pliable dough. Roll out on a lightly floured surface and use to line a deep, 23cm (9in) loose-bottomed, lightly greased, tart tin. Prick the pastry base all over with a fork. Line with greaseproof paper, fill with baking beans. and bake blind in the oven for 20 minutes.

For the filling, beat the eggs, cream and seasoning together, then gradually combine this with the cheeses. Pour into the pastry case and bake for a further 30-35 minutes until golden.

Serve with warm Grape Chutney (see page 154) and a crisp green salad.

Opposite: Goat's Cheese and Parmesan Tart served with warm Grape Chutney

AUTUMN

I am starting off autumn with two squash dishes as I really love this vegetable and it epitomizes the feel of the season with its wonderful colours: vivid oranges, bright and pale yellows and soft greens. You can buy all the squash you need, but they are easy and satisfying to grow, too.

ROAST SQUASH SERVED WITH CHILLI SATAY SAUCE

This dish came about when I asked one of our chefs, Simon, to jazz up a tray of roast squash and he had the inspired idea of adding chilli to a satay sauce!

For 4 people, take a selection of squash. Peel and cut into crescent shapes by halving, quartering and so on until the shapes are about 4cm (1½in) across. Remove and discard the seeds. Place in a baking tin, sprinkle with sea salt and freshly ground black pepper and drizzle cold-pressed olive oil over them. Then roast the squash pieces in a pre-heated oven at 200°C/400°F/Gas Mark 6 for 20 minutes.

While the squash is roasting, make the sauce using the following ingredients:

1 tablespoon olive oil
1 small onion, finely chopped
55g (2oz) brown sugar
2 fresh red chillies, finely chopped
1 tablespoon peanut butter
1 tablespoon tahini
400ml (14fl oz) coconut milk
handful of fresh basil, chopped

Heat the oil in a shallow frying pan, add the onion and cook until lightly browned, stirring occasionally. Add the sugar and stir vigorously, then add the chillies and cook for 1 minute, stirring. Add the peanut butter to the mixture and work together, while slowly adding the tahini followed by the coconut milk. Simmer for 10 minutes, but keep stirring to prevent the sauce from sticking. As you take the pan from the heat, throw in the chopped basil and pour onto the roast squash.

We serve this with a fragrant rice from Thailand, but a basmati rice cooked with sticks of lemon grass suspended in the well-seasoned water, will taste wonderful as well.

Left: Cut the squash into crescent shapes and place on a baking tray. Opposite: Roast Squash served with Chilli Satay Sauce and fragrant rice.

PUMPKIN SOUP WITH HERB AND GARLIC-TOPPED FOCACCIA

For this soup, choose the really bright orange-fleshed pumpkins to give the soup a vibrant colour.

SERVES 4

4 tablespoons butter

1 onion, chopped

1 clove garlic, crushed

900g (2lb) pumpkins peeled, deseeded and roughly chopped

850ml (1½ pints) vegetable stock

sea salt and freshly ground black pepper

600ml (1 pint) double cream or Greek yoghurt

chopped fresh parsley, to garnish

Melt the butter in a large saucepan, add the onion and fry until soft, stirring occasionally, then add the garlic and pumpkin and mix well. Lightly sauté for a few minutes, then pour in the stock. Bring to the boil, then reduce the heat, cover and simmer for about 20 minutes, or until the vegetables are tender, stirring occasionally.

Remove the pan from the heat and cool slightly. Reserve 4 pieces of pumpkin for garnish, then purée the remaining pumpkin mixture in a blender or food processor until smooth.

Return to the rinsed-out pan and season with salt and pepper. Reheat gently before serving. If you want to add double cream or Greek yoghurt, whisk about 600ml (1 pint) into the soup now. Reheat gently, without boiling, before serving.

To serve, ladle the soup into warm soup bowls, then place a whole piece of reserved pumpkin in the centre of each bowl and sprinkle with a little chopped parsley. A little cream or Greek yoghurt can be swirled in at the last minute to give a marbled effect.

Accompany with focaccia bread, sliced through horizontally and spread with garlic and herb butter, then grilled until bubbling.

VEGETARIAN MOUSSAKA

SERVES 4

3 aubergines, sliced into rounds about 1cm (½in) thick

sea salt and freshly ground black pepper

4 tablespoons olive oil

225g (8oz) onions, sliced

2 cloves garlic, crushed

450g (1lb) meatless mince (see page 50)

75ml (2½ fl oz) red wine

2 tablespoons tomato purée

1 tablespoon chopped fresh parsley

1 teaspoon ground cinnamon

FOR THE SAUCE:

85g (3oz) butter

85g (3oz) plain flour

600ml (1 pint) milk

55g (2oz) cheddar cheese, grated

1 teaspoon freshly grated nutmeg

2 eggs, beaten

Sprinkle the aubergines with salt and put them in a colander, then place a plate on top of them and a heavy weight on top of that. Set aside for about 1 hour.

Preheat the oven to 180°C/350°F/Gas Mark 4. Heat 2 tablespoons oil in a pan, add the onions and garlic and fry for about 5 minutes to soften them, stirring occasionally. Add the meatless mince to the pan. Mix together the wine, tomato purée, parsley, cinnamon and seasoning, then add to the pan. Stir well and leave to simmer on a gentle heat for about 15 minutes, stirring occasionally.

Pat the aubergines dry with absorbent kitchen paper. In a separate pan, heat the remaining oil and fry the aubergine slices until golden brown on each side, then place on absorbent kitchen paper to drain. When you have fried all the aubergines, line the bottom of a casserole dish with aubergines. Spread some meatless mince mixture on the top, add another layer of aubergines, then meatless mince and continue until you have layered all the aubergines and meatless mince, ending with a layer of aubergines.

To make the sauce, melt the butter in a saucepan and stir in the flour until smooth, then gradually add the milk and heat gently, stirring continuously, to make a traditional béchamel (white) sauce. When you have a smooth, thick sauce, stir in the cheese, nutmeg and seasoning. Remove the pan from the heat and allow to cool slightly, then add the beaten eggs, whisking them into the sauce as you go. Pour the sauce over the aubergines and bake in the oven for 1 hour until the top is golden.

Serve with Country Bread (see page 22) and a green salad with a vinaigrette dressing.

WILD MUSHROOM RISOTTO

We like to use a mixture of dried and fresh wild and domestic mushrooms. If that sounds complicated, the exact mix really does not matter that much except that it is nice to have at least some dried mushrooms because the water in which they are soaked becomes a wonderful tasting liquid. The secret of a good risotto is to have a lot of rich stock available and ladle it slowly into the simmering rice. You need to be on hand throughout the cooking process – it is not a dish you can leave.

SERVES 4

40g (1½oz) dried porcini mushrooms
6 tablespoons olive oil
2 cloves garlic, finely chopped
115g (4oz) fresh chestnut or button mushrooms, sliced
2 tablespoons chopped fresh flat-leaf parsley
2 tablespoons fresh basil leaves, torn into pieces
sea salt and freshly ground black pepper
115g (4oz) butter
1 onion, chopped
225g (8oz) risotto rice
600ml (1 pint) hot vegetable stock
115g (4oz) fresh mixed wild mushrooms, chopped
600ml (1 pint) white wine
115g (4oz) freshly grated parmesan cheese
chopped fresh parsley, to garnish

Soak the dried mushrooms in 300ml (½ pint) boiling water in a bowl for 15 minutes, then remove the mushrooms using a slotted spoon and place them on a plate. Strain the soaking liquid through a fine sieve or a piece of muslin as wild mushrooms tend to be quite gritty. Reserve the strained soaking liquid as it has a rich, intense flavour. Wash the dried mushrooms again to make sure there is no grit left, then pat them dry and chop them.

In a large, heavy-based sauté or frying pan, heat 4 tablespoons oil, then add the garlic and chopped porcini mushrooms. Cook, stirring, until the garlic starts to brown, then add the chestnut or button mushrooms. Cook for a further 10 minutes, stirring occasionally, then pour in the reserved mushroom juices. Remove from the heat, stir in the herbs and seasoning, then set aside.

In a separate heavy-based frying pan, melt half the butter and the remaining oil and fry the onion gently for 5 minutes until soft, stirring occasionally. Add the rice and stir into the butter and onion mixture, cooking for a further few minutes until coated. Add the mushroom and herb mixture and cook for a further 5 minutes, stirring occasionally.

Add two ladlefuls of stock and the fresh wild mushrooms and cook over a medium heat, stirring all the time. When the rice has absorbed the liquid, add another ladleful of stock. Continue gradually adding the stock, a ladleful at a time, until the rice has absorbed all the liquid, then gradually add the wine and cook until the rice has absorbed all the liquid and it is tender. Adjust the seasoning, stir in the remaining butter and serve immediately, sprinkled with grated parmesan and garnished with chopped parsley.

A bubbling stockpot for the best risottos in town.

ROOT VEGETABLE STEW WITH CHEESE RAREBITS

SERVES 4

FOR THE STEW:

2 onions

4 sticks celery

2 turnips

1 pumpkin, deseeded

6 parsnips

4 potatoes

2 sweet potatoes

2 tablespoons olive oil

2 cloves garlic, crushed

2 tablespoons chopped fresh mixed herbs
  such as thyme, rosemary and sage
  or 2 teaspoons dried mixed herbs

sea salt and freshly ground black pepper

Wash, peel and coarsely dice all the vegetables and set aside. Heat the oil in a large, heavy-based saucepan and gently fry the onions and celery until the colour starts to change, stirring occasionally.

Add the garlic, herbs and seasoning, then add 1.2 litres (2 pints) water. Bring to the boil, cover, then reduce the heat and simmer slowly for about 30 minutes, until you have a tasty stock.

Stir in the remaining diced vegetables, return to a gentle boil, then continue to simmer until they are soft, but not breaking up. I like my vegetables *al dente*, but this is my preference – we have two cooking times in my household! Serve with cheese rarebits and garnish with flat parsley.

CHEESE RAREBITS

To make the cheese rarebits, lay thick slices of organic vegetarian cheddar cheese onto pieces of country bread, dot with a little butter and place under the grill for about 2 minutes, until golden brown. Serve piping hot and sizzling. It is important to choose organic cheese to avoid genetically modified rennet.

WINTER

The winter harvest lacks the exuberance and variety of summer but it does provide a wonderful opportunity to combine all manner of dried beans and pulses with root vegetables. Liven up these dishes with herbs and spices and eat with crusty bread and real butter and you will never regret living in a cold climate again!

ROAST ONION SOUP WITH HERB AND CHEESE DUMPLINGS

SERVES 4 AS A LUNCH DISH

FOR THE SOUP:

5 onions

900g (2lb) tomatoes, skinned
  or canned chopped tomatoes (add to blender)

2 carrots

4 cloves garlic

2 tablespoons olive oil

sea salt and freshly ground black pepper

850ml (1½ pints) vegetable stock

FOR THE DUMPLINGS:

115g (4oz) curd cheese

55g (2oz) fresh breadcrumbs

1 tablespoon each of chopped fresh chives,
  parsley and coriander

1 large egg, beaten

Preheat the oven to 200°C/400°F/Gas Mark 6. Peel the onions and cut them in half, halve the tomatoes, split the carrots in half, split the unpeeled garlic and place the

Opposite: Root Vegetable Stew with Cheese Rarebits

prepared vegetables in a roasting tin. Drizzle with oil, season with salt and pepper and roast in the oven for about 30 minutes, until soft and brown.

Meanwhile, make the dumplings by mashing the curd cheese with a fork in a bowl. Mix in the breadcrumbs, herbs and seasoning. Add the egg and mix well, then shape into small nut-sized pieces, place on a plate and chill for 15 minutes.

Remove the roast vegetables from the oven and cool slightly, then skin the garlic. Place the vegetables in a blender or food processor with all the cooking juices, add the stock and purée until smooth. Pass through a sieve into a clean pan and reheat the soup until simmering, stirring occasionally.

Add the dumplings and poach in the soup for 3-4 minutes. Serve immediately.

LLANGLOFFAN FARMHOUSE

This cheese is hand-crafted using traditional equipment and methods. It is best described as having a rich, yet slightly dry, almost crumbly texture that melts in the mouth. The textured rind is stone-coloured, showing the imprint of the cloth in which it is moulded.

"Say Wales and then farmhouse cheese, and people in the know will now say Llangloffan" wrote Pamela Westland in her book *British Country Cheeses*. Twenty-two years ago, Leon Downey packed his viola and headed off to Wales with his wife Joan and young family, to settle at Llangloffan Farmhouse. Leon was once co-principle viola player in the Hallé Orchestra, under Sir John Barbirolli but, although the financial rewards were high, constant travelling meant that he was not seeing enough of his wife and family. The Hallé's loss is our gain.

What makes his cheese different? It is made from unpasteurized milk from cows which have grazed solely on grass on which no sort of chemical is used. The cheese itself is made by hand, using original liquid starter cultures and incorporating the best of traditional methods.

Left: Farming organically is not limited to the food the animals eat – stringent controls also surround the use of medication, for example. Opposite: The rind of Llangloffan Farmhouse Cheese is stone-coloured and bears the imprint of the cloth in which it is moulded.

STUFFED CABBAGE LEAVES WITH A SPICY TOMATO SAUCE

SERVES 4

FOR THE STUFFED CABBAGE LEAVES:

175g (6oz) long or short grain rice

sea salt and freshly ground black pepper

1 bouquet garni (optional)

1 tablespoon olive oil

1 onion, chopped

1 stick celery, chopped

1 clove garlic, crushed

115g (4oz) mushrooms, chopped

55g (2oz) cashew nuts, chopped

8 outer savoy cabbage leaves

FOR THE SPICY TOMATO SAUCE:

1 quantity basic tomato sauce (see page 40)

1 teaspoon grated fresh root ginger

1 teaspoon ground chilli powder

1 teaspoon ground cloves

Bring 450ml (16fl oz) water to the boil in a large saucepan. Add the rice, a good pinch of salt and the bouquet garni, if using, and cook for about 45 minutes, until the rice is soft. Drain well.

Meanwhile, heat the oil in a pan, add the onion, celery and garlic and fry until soft and lightly browned, stirring occasionally. Add the mushrooms and continue to cook for another 5 minutes. Stir in the cashew nuts and drained rice, mixing well. Remove from the heat and set aside.

Opposite:
Stuffed Cabbage Leaves with a Spicy Tomato Sauce

Blanch the cabbage leaves by adding them to half a pan of boiling, salted water and simmer them for 2 minutes. Drain and rinse under the cold tap, then drain again.

Preheat the oven to 190°C/375°F/Gas Mark 5. Divide the rice mixture evenly between the cabbage leaves, rolling each cabbage leaf around the filling to make a fat parcel. Place the rolls in a shallow ovenproof dish, cover and bake for 30 minutes.

To make the tomato sauce, follow the recipe on page 40 and add the ginger, chilli powder and ground cloves. Serve the cooked stuffed cabbage leaves with the tomato sauce poured over the top.

CARROT, MUSHROOM, SESAME AND GINGER OVEN ROAST

SERVES 4-6

25g (1oz) butter, plus extra for dotting

2 cloves garlic, crushed

1 onion, chopped

450g (1lb) mushrooms, chopped

140g (5oz) grated carrots

55g (2oz) fresh root ginger, peeled and finely chopped

55g (2oz) sesame seeds

5 eggs, beaten

140g (5oz) fresh whole-wheat breadcrumbs

140g (5oz) cheddar cheese, grated

1 teaspoon chopped fresh thyme

1 teaspoon chopped fresh basil

sea salt and freshly ground black pepper

Preheat the oven to 180°C/350°F/Gas Mark 4. Grease a 450g (1lb) loaf tin and set aside. Melt 25g (1oz) butter in a pan and mix in the garlic. Add the onion and sauté until soft and lightly browned, stirring occasionally. Remove from the heat and add all the other ingredients, saving half of the breadcrumbs and cheese for the top, and mix well.

Spoon into the prepared loaf tin. Sprinkle with the

Opposite: Mixed Bean Stew with Herb Dumplings

remaining breadcrumbs and cheese mixed together. Dot with butter. Cover with foil and bake in the oven for 30 minutes, then uncover and bake for a further 5 minutes until browned. Turn out onto a plate and serve either hot with a dressing of yoghurt and herbs or cold with salad.

MIXED BEAN STEW WITH HERB DUMPLINGS

Dried beans are winter staples throughout the world, the Spaniards favour chickpeas, the Italians go for cannellini and the French for their beloved haricot. So choose whatever you fancy, but try to get a mix of colours. The key to cooking dried beans is to soak them sufficiently – check the packet for optimum soak times which vary depending on variety.

SERVES 4

FOR THE BEAN STEW:

115g (4oz) dried chickpeas, soaked

115g (4oz) dried white beans such as haricot beans, soaked

115g (4oz) dried red beans such as aduki beans, soaked

115g (4oz) dried green beans such as flageolet beans, soaked

2 tablespoons olive oil

2 onions, chopped

2 cloves garlic, crushed

two 225g (8oz) cans chopped tomatoes

125ml (4fl oz) red wine

125ml (4fl oz) vegetable stock

sea salt and freshly ground black pepper

225g (8oz) carrots, sliced

225g (8oz) parsnips, chopped

FOR THE DUMPLINGS:

115g (4oz) self-raising flour

pinch of sea salt and freshly ground black pepper

pinch of dry mustard

1 tablespoon fresh parsley, finely chopped

1 tablespoon fresh sage, finely chopped

55g (2oz) butter, diced

Start by making the bean stew. Soak the beans overnight in plenty of water, then rinse and drain thoroughly. Heat the oil in a large pan and fry the onions and garlic until golden, stirring occasionally. Stir in the pre-soaked beans and cook this mixture until slightly browned, stirring occasionally. Stir in the tomatoes, wine, stock and seasoning, bring to the boil, then reduce the heat and simmer for 40 minutes, stirring occasionally.

Meanwhile, make the dumplings. Sift the flour into a bowl, add the salt, pepper, parsley, sage and mustard, then rub in the butter. Bind the ingredients together with water to make a slightly sticky dough. Lightly flour your hands and roll the dough into 8-12 balls.

Add the carrots and parsnips to the bean stew and stir to mix. Pop the dumplings into the boiling stew and simmer, covered, for 20 minutes. Check to see that all the vegetables are tender before serving.

CHICKPEAS IN A SPICY TOMATO AND CORIANDER SAUCE

SERVES 4

450g (1lb) dried chickpeas, soaked
115g (4oz) onions, finely chopped
2 cloves garlic, crushed
1-2 small red chillies, finely chopped
55g (2oz) celery, finely chopped
115g (4oz) carrots, finely chopped
3-4 tablespoons olive oil
sea salt and freshly ground black pepper
300ml (½ pint) vegetable stock
400g (14oz) can chopped tomatoes, drained
1 bayleaf
2 tablespoons finely chopped fresh coriander, plus extra
   to garnish

If you do not have time to soak the chickpeas overnight, you can boil them in water for 2 hours then leave them to stand in the hot water for 2 hours. Whichever method you are using, strain the chickpeas, cover with fresh water (and fresh herbs if you have some to hand), bring to the boil and simmer until soft, which will take between 30-40 minutes. Drain well.

Take a large, heavy-based pan and sauté the onions, garlic, chillies, celery and carrots in the olive oil for about 5 minutes, stirring occasionally. Season and add the vegetable stock. Cover and simmer for 15 minutes, then add the chickpeas, tomatoes, bayleaf and coriander and cook until the consistency is like a stew, stirring occasionally. Serve in bowls on a sweet potato mash or with couscous and sprinkle fresh chopped coriander on top.

Left: Oven-dried tomatoes (see page 148)
Opposite: Chickpeas in a Spicy Tomato and Coriander Sauce.

MUSHROOM STROGANOFF

This is a great dish, which is quick and easy to make yet is smart enough for any dinner party.

SERVES 4

2 tablespoons butter

1 onion, chopped

225g (8oz) mushrooms, chopped

600ml (1 pint) sour cream

300ml (½ pint) Greek yoghurt

3 tablespoons red wine

2 teaspoons tamari

1 teaspoon chopped fresh dill

pinch of paprika

sea salt and freshly ground black pepper

spring onions or shallots, to garnish

Melt the butter in a pan, add the onion and cook until they are soft and browning, stirring occasionally. Add the mushrooms and cook until soft, stirring occasionally. Add all the remaining ingredients and mix well. Bring gently to the boil, then simmer, uncovered, for about 30 minutes, stirring occasionally.

Opposite: Hot and crisp Breakfast Potatoes

Serve with cooked fresh noodles (see Nouilles page 42) and steamed vegetables. Assemble on plates and scatter finely chopped spring onions or shallots over them to garnish.

OVEN POTATOES OR POMMES LYONNAISE

Lay thinly sliced potatoes in a greased ovenproof dish and pour over some well-seasoned vegetable stock. Cover and cook in a preheated oven at 180°C/350°F/Gas Mark 4 for about 40 minutes, then remove the lid and dot with butter. Increase the oven temperature to 200°C/400°F/Gas Mark 6 and cook for a further 10 minutes to brown.

OVEN WEDGE CHIPS

Preheat the oven to 200°C/400°F/Gas Mark 6. Scrub the potatoes and cut each into 8 wedges. Pour about 3 tablespoons olive oil into a roasting tin, add the potatoes and turn them in the oil to coat all over. Season well and sprinkle with either chopped garlic and herbs or alternatively spice them up with chilli powder. Bake in the oven for 40-50 minutes until cooked and crisp.

FONDANT POTATOES

This is a very rich way of roasting potatoes. Traditionally it uses butter, but you can use olive oil if you prefer. Ideally you need small new potatoes, but otherwise cut larger ones into quarters. Place in a heavy-based pan and add 25g (1oz) butter or olive oil (you could use half butter and half olive oil) for each 450g (1lb) potatoes. Cover the pan and cook over a gentle flame, shaking the pan from time to time to make sure they don't stick. Turn after 15 minutes and cook for a further 10 minutes, salting to taste before serving.

BREAKFAST POTATOES

We use a simpler version of fondant potatoes to make our breakfast potatoes. Boil the potatoes in their skins and when cooked, but still firm, cut into small pieces. Sauté with olive oil or sunflower oil in a wok until crisp and golden brown. Add a sprinkling of sea salt and serve.

Meat
as it is meant to be

Nowadays, most of the chicken, pork and beef we eat is produced by intensive farming. This means that the animals live in crowded, stressful conditions, that they are routinely dosed with antibiotics and growth-promoting hormones (which give a faster turnover of animals) and that they are fed unnatural foods, which may, for example, contain the ground-up carcasses of other animals as we know from the BSE scandal. Organic meat brings back the succulent flavours that I remember from my childhood. It is undoubtedly more expensive but just remember it is meat that is meant to be derived from animals that have lived as they are meant to live.

For me, chickens or 'hens' as my mother always called them, are evocative of the weekly chore of cleaning out the hen house and collecting warm eggs from nesting boxes. During the war, most people kept chickens in their back gardens and it is no secret that we war babies have been an incredibly healthy generation partly due, I am sure, to eating our own organically grown home produce. In those days, a close relationship with the animals that fed us was the natural thing.

When one of my mother's hens fell from the big apple tree where she had been perching, my mother strapped her leg to a pencil until it set and kept her in the outside lavatory, spending at least half an hour each day nursing her because the hen's bottom was raw with sitting! This may have been going a bit far, especially considering that she did eventually end up in the pot, but when I visited a commercial battery farm a few years ago, the sights I saw there convinced me that there is no greater example of man's inhumanity to animals than intensive, large scale, commercial farming. The price of cheap meat is paid in suffering. This is why we only use organic meat reared by traditional methods.

Organic hens range freely in a large field (above) before retiring to their luxurious hen-house (left) at the Hardwick Estate, Reading.

THE HARDWICK ESTATE

The Hardwick Estate near Reading in South Oxfordshire is the home of Julian and Elizabeth Rose. Julian inherited this stunning Elizabethan estate consisting of 350 acres of farmland, with 500 further acres of forestry, when his elder brother died unexpectedly. Julian and Elizabeth had to decide whether or not to leave their theatre company in Antwerp, Belgium, and return to England to take up the reins of a large and impoverished estate. It was not a decision taken lightly: the economic vista was extremely unattractive. The run-down house – where his mother still lived – had been divided and let to tenants, while the outbuildings and Victorian market garden were little more than ruins. The farm had been unviable for many years.

They decided to give it a go, but took the decision to farm organically. This meant that at first they could not use a large part of the farm, which had been sprayed with pesticides. However, there were meadows untouched by chemicals and one of their first purchases was a herd of Guernsey cows. Julian was determined not to pasteurize this pure creamy milk and could not, therefore, sell it into the usual milk outlets. Undeterred, he acquired a milk float and sold his milk direct to the customers around the streets of Reading.

Gradually the Roses rebuilt the outhouses, restored the house and cottages on the Estate and converted the farm to organic principles. This alone would have been a mammoth achievement but it was taken a step further. The Roses invited individuals to manage and run sections of the farm as separate enterprises because they felt this to be an appropriate, sustainable and fulfilling method of land management. Their objective was to foster a sense of community which would benefit both the people and the environment.

Above and left: The table poultry and dairy enterprises at the Hardwick Estate. Opposite: Carefully raised stock has earned Graig Farm awards for their flavoursome organic meat.

There are now many different enterprises running parallel with the Estate management at Hardwick including pig farming, table poultry, a dairy herd, beef, sheep, arable land, hens for laying and fruit and vegetable gardens. There is also an award-winning farm shop, The Old Dairy, run by Elizabeth, which stocks all the produce from the farm and includes smoked venison from deer that range free in the forest.

GRAIG FARM

Graig Farm in Powys, Wales, is probably the largest supplier of organic meat and fish in the UK. They are also the sole importers for St. Helena's fish, the only wild fish to be certified by the Soil Association (see page 114). Graig Farm offers a wide choice of award-winning British meats, such as the Welsh Black or Hereford Beef, Welsh Mountain Lamb and Gloucester Old Spot or Wessex Saddleback Pigs. All are reared on organic pastures and by humane farming methods. They are then traditionally matured to give an outstanding flavour. Graig Farm also supplies a wide range of game, such as venison, rabbit and boar.

POULTRY

When I was growing up, we had chicken once a week – and we were lucky. Chicken was a luxury food – often eaten only at Christmas and special occasions – not deep frozen, white and insipid.

LEMON-MARINATED BREASTS OF CHICKEN

This first chicken recipe is one of our most popular and it happened by chance when Lizzie was dreaming up a new lunch special.

SERVES 4

4 boneless chicken breasts, skinned
   (we use whole chickens and take the breasts off. In order not to have any waste, the legs and thighs are then used for other dishes and the carcasses boiled up with celery, onions and herbs to make a stock)
2 red chillies, chopped (optional)
8 tablespoons lemon juice
sprinkling of chopped fresh rosemary (optional)
sea salt and freshly ground black pepper
2 tablespoons cold-pressed olive oil
4 tablespoons brown sugar

Place the chicken breasts in a shallow, non-metallic dish. Pour over the lemon juice, sprinkle with rosemary and red chillies, if using, and season with salt and pepper. Turn the chicken breasts to coat them all over. Cover and leave to marinate in the refrigerator for at least 3 hours, but preferably overnight.

Heat the oil in a frying pan over a high heat and pan-fry the chicken breasts, turning frequently, until they are brown and cooked through. This should take about 5 minutes. Pour in the juices from the marinade and let it

bubble. Add the sugar and stir until dissolved and starting to caramelize.

Serve on a bed of lightly cooked spinach with potatoes that have been sautéed in butter with chopped garlic and fresh parsley.

TAJINE OF CHICKEN WITH OLIVES AND PRESERVED LEMONS

Preserved lemons are widely used in Moroccan cooking and are one of their great specialities (see page 150). In this dish, the sweet taste of these lemons compliments the slightly bitter taste of the olives.

SERVES 4

2-3 tablespoons cold-pressed olive oil
1 onion, finely chopped
3 cloves garlic, crushed
1 teaspoon ground ginger
1 teaspoon ground cinnamon
1 large pinch of saffron strands
sea salt and freshly ground black pepper
1 chicken, approx. 1.5kg (3lb 5oz) in weight
700ml (1¼ pints) chicken stock
   (see recipe on page 16)
125g (4½oz) natural black pitted olives
2 preserved lemons, roughly chopped
1 bunch of fresh coriander, finely chopped
1 bunch of fresh parsley, finely chopped

Heat the oil in a frying pan, add the onion and fry gently until soft and brown. Add the garlic, ginger, cinnamon, saffron, salt and pepper and continue to cook, stirring until the mixture starts to release its pungent smells.

Place the chicken in a deep, flameproof casserole or saucepan and spread the onion and spice mixture over it. Pour in the stock and bring to the boil. Cover with a lid,

Opposite: Lemon-marinated Breasts of Chicken

reduce the heat to low and simmer for about 1¼ hours, turning the chicken two or three times.

Add the olives, preserved lemons, coriander and parsley. Cover once again and continue to cook for a further 15 minutes, or until the chicken is very tender.

Taste the sauce and if it needs to be stronger, place the chicken on a hot serving dish, cover and keep warm, while you reduce the juices by boiling them over a high heat, until you have a thick, aromatic sauce. Tilt the pan and remove and discard the excess fat from the sauce before pouring the sauce over the chicken.

Serve on a bed of cooked couscous or rice.

ROAST DUCK WITH APRICOT SAUCE

SERVES 4

175g (6oz) dried apricots, soaked
850ml (1½ pints) hot vegetable stock
2 tablespoons balsamic vinegar
1 tablespoon brown sugar
sea salt and freshly ground black pepper
1 duck about 1.3kg (3lb) in weight
2 tablespoons olive oil
2 tablespoons butter

Place the apricots in a bowl, pour over the stock and leave to soak until the apricots are soft – this will take at least 2 hours.

Preheat the oven to 200°C/400°F/Gas Mark 6. Place the apricots and stock in a blender or food processor with the vinegar, sugar and seasoning and blend until smooth. Pour into a pan and bring to the boil stirring occasionally. Lower to a medium heat and continue to stir until the sauce reduces and becomes thick and syrupy. Keep warm.

Meanwhile, cut diagonally across the body of the duck. Heat the oil and butter in a heavy-based, ovenproof frying pan until smoking. Add the duck and sear its skin all over until crisp, turning frequently, then place the pan in the oven and bake for about 20 minutes, or until cooked and tender. The duck is cooked when it is pierced between the leg and the body and the juices run clear.

Carve the duck, place in a warm serving dish and pour the apricot sauce over. Serve with rice, mashed potatoes or lentils.

Left: Breast of Chicken marinating in lemon (see page 86). Opposite: Roast Duck with Apricot Sauce served with lentils

BEEF

The rearing of beef in the industrialized world has become the most debated food issue of our time. You can read more about it in the last chapter of this book. Suffice it to say that by choosing organically fed and traditionally reared beef, you can safeguard yourself from the repercussions of bad farming, and boycott inhumane practices.

STEAK & KIDNEY PIE

We use a shortcrust pastry to cover this traditional English pie.

SERVES 4

For the pie filling:

225g (8oz) whole lamb's or pig's kidneys

25g (1oz) plain flour

sea salt and freshly ground black pepper

900g (2lb) stewing steak, cut into 2.5cm (1in) cubes

3 tablespoons olive oil

1 large onion, chopped

2 cloves garlic, crushed

225ml (8fl oz) beef stock

125ml (4fl oz) red wine or beer

2 teaspoons Worcestershire sauce

For the shortcrust pastry:

225g (8oz) plain flour

pinch of salt

115g (4oz) butter

1 egg yolk, beaten, to glaze

Make the pie filling. Wash the kidneys and remove and discard the membranes and hard white cores. Chop the flesh into 2.5cm (1in) pieces. Place the flour and seasoning in a large, clean plastic or freezer bag, add the beef and kidney pieces and toss until they are coated in flour.

Heat a little oil in a large pan. Add the pieces of meat to the pan a few at a time and cook until browned all over, stirring. Remove the pieces of meat as they brown, using a slotted spoon and place on a plate. Add more oil to the pan if necessary and continue cooking the meat in batches until all the meat is browned.

Reduce the heat, add the onion to the pan and cook over a low heat until soft and browning, stirring occasionally. Add the garlic and cook for a further 1 minute before adding the stock, wine or beer, Worcestershire sauce and seasoning. Add the browned meat, stir to mix, then bring to the boil. Reduce the heat, cover and simmer for 2 hours or until the meat is tender, stirring occasionally.

Meanwhile, make the pastry. Sift the flour with the salt into a large bowl. Cut the butter into small pieces and add to the flour. Rub the butter into the flour with your fingertips until it resembles breadcrumbs, then add 8 teaspoons cold water and stir around with a blunt knife until it forms a dough. Collect together with your hands, turn onto a floured surface and knead quickly for a couple of minutes to give a smooth, firm dough. Wrap the dough loosely in a clean tea towel or greaseproof paper and refrigerate for about 15 minutes.

Preheat the oven to 200°C/400°F/Gas Mark 6. Spoon the meat mixture into a 1.2 litre (2 pint) pie dish and place a pie funnel in the centre. Roll out the pastry on a lightly floured surface to form a circle 5cm (2in) larger than the top of the pie dish. Trim a 2.5cm (1in) piece from all round the edge of the pastry circle and lay this on the dampened edge of the pie dish. Place the whole pastry circle on top, making a slit in the centre for the pie funnel to go through and to allow steam to escape.

Trim and flute the pastry edges and brush all over with beaten egg yolk to glaze. Bake in the oven for about 40 minutes, covering the pastry with foil if it browns too quickly. Serve with broccoli or plain mashed potatoes.

Opposite: Steak and Kidney Pie. This is an example of one of Lizzie's generous portions!

BEEF STEWED WITH JUNIPER BERRIES AND ORANGE ZEST

Because organic beef can be expensive, cheaper cuts such as topside are a very sensible choice. These cuts can be transformed into classic beef stews or rich casseroles using seasonal vegetables – we add juniper berries and the grated zest and juice of an orange to lift this dish.

SERVES 4

1 tablespoon plain flour
sea salt and freshly ground black pepper
900g (2lb) topside of beef, cut into 2.5cm (1in) cubes
2 tablespoons olive oil
55g (2oz) butter
2 onions, chopped
1 tablespoon juniper berries (dried or fresh), flattened
    with the blade of a knife
finely grated zest and juice of 1 orange
2 cloves garlic, crushed
225g (8oz) parsnips, diced

225g (8oz) turnips, diced
1 teaspoon chopped fresh thyme
1 teaspoon chopped fresh sage
600ml (1 pint) boiling beef stock

Preheat the oven to 170°C/325°F/Gas Mark 3. Place the flour and seasoning in a large, clean plastic bag (make sure it's clean inside if recycled from the shopping!) add the beef cubes and toss until they are thoroughly coated in flour. Set aside.

Heat the oil and butter in a heavy-based ovenproof pan, add the onions and cook until soft, stirring occasionally. Add the beef and cook quickly, stirring, until the meat is sealed all over.

Add the juniper berries, orange zest and juice, garlic, parsnips, turnips and herbs. Finally pour on the boiling stock and stir to mix, then cover and cook in the oven for 2-3 hours or until the meat is cooked and tender, stirring once or twice. The flour will thicken the gravy of the casserole and this can then be served straight from the pan. Serve with sweet potato mash.

FILLET OF BEEF WITH BEARNAISE SAUCE

For this dish, you can either use fillet steak or, for a special treat, a *chateaubriand* steak which is cut from the centre and thickest part of the fillet and weighs about 350g (12oz) – enough for two people. With fillet take a 175g (6oz) steak for each person and pan-fry in a mixture of butter and olive oil on a high heat until the beef is cooked to your liking. For a *chateaubriand*, brush the meat with olive oil, sprinkle with a little coarse sea salt and freshly ground black pepper and roast in a very hot oven at 230°C/450°F/Gas Mark 8 for about 15 minutes. Serve with Béarnaise Sauce (see page 94) and Fondant Potatoes or Oven Wedge Chips (see page 80).

Left: The butcher at work at Graig Farm.
Opposite: Fillet of Beef with Béarnaise Sauce
and Fondant Potatoes

BEARNAISE SAUCE

This is my very favourite sauce and although traditionally made with tarragon, you can use other herbs. Replace the tarragon with dill and try it with salmon or trout.

SERVES 6

    5 tablespoons white wine or cider vinegar
    1 shallot or ½ onion, finely chopped
    3 egg yolks
    175g (6oz) butter, cut into 8 pieces
    2 tablespoons chopped fresh tarragon
    sea salt and freshly ground black pepper

Place the vinegar in a pan, add the shallot or onion, bring to the boil, then simmer until the liquid has reduced to about 2 tablespoons. Remove from the heat, allow to cool and strain into a mixing bowl. Beat the egg yolks into the reduced vinegar one at a time.

Place the bowl over a pan of warm water, (or use a bain marie), put the pan over a low heat and, stirring constantly with a wooden spoon, add the butter piece by piece, until the sauce is thick. Stir in the chopped tarragon leaves and season to taste.

Above: Harvested beetroot – one of the most under-rated of all the root vegetables.
Opposite: Lamb Shanks braised in Cider with Glazed Onions & Beetroot

LAMB

Many people ask me why lamb isn't automatically organic since the animals graze on untouched hillsides. Well, of course, this is true up to a point although a lot of pasture lands are sprayed. The main problem with lamb is actually the sheep dip, which contains heavy doses of pesticides. This dip is not used on organic lambs.

LAMB SHANKS BRAISED IN CIDER WITH GLAZED ONIONS & BEETROOT

The shank is the bony end of the leg, which is cut off and sold separately. It is very good value – important when buying organic – and extremely tender when braised slowly with excellent flavour.

SERVES 4

FOR THE LAMB SHANKS:
    4 lamb shanks
    600ml (1 pint) cider
    300ml (½ pint) meat stock
    1 onion, cut into quarters
    2 carrots, thickly sliced
    1 stick celery, sliced
    1 bouquet garni
    sea salt and freshly ground black pepper
    8 medium-sized potatoes or 16 new
       potatoes, scrubbed

FOR THE GLAZED ONIONS AND BEETROOT:
    1 tablespoon olive oil
    1 onion, sliced into thin matchsticks
    1 beetroot, cooked and sliced into small chunks
    2 tablespoons brown sugar

Preheat the oven to 170°C/325°F/Gas Mark 3. Place the lamb shanks into a large baking dish with the cider, stock, onion, carrots, celery, bouquet garni and seasoning. Roast in the oven for 1½ hours. Add the potatoes 30 minutes before the end of the cooking time and continue roasting until cooked. If the potatoes are large you may need to parboil them for approximately 10 minutes before adding them to the lamb.

Remove the lamb and vegetables from the pan and place on a warm serving plate. Cover and keep hot. Remove and discard the bouquet garni. Place the pan on top of the stove, bring the juices to the boil and boil rapidly to reduce and thicken. If you like a thick sauce, you can add some *beurre manié* (15g/½oz butter worked into 25g/1oz plain flour with your fingertips and then whisked quickly into the boiling liquid).

To make the glazed onions and beetroot, heat the oil in a pan and gently fry the onions until browning, then add the beetroot and fry for a further 2 minutes, stirring occasionally. Add the sugar and cook until the sugar has mingled with the juices of the vegetables and they have a glazed appearance, stirring occasionally.

Serve the cooked lamb shanks on individual plates with the vegetables and gravy round the meat. Serve with the glazed onions and beetroot spooned on top of the lamb.

Opposite: Herb-stuffed, Pot-roasted Lamb

HERB-STUFFED, POT-ROASTED LAMB

This is a good joint for a family Sunday lunch as a boned shoulder of lamb will weigh about 1.8kg (4lb).

SERVES 6-8

3 handfuls of chopped fresh mixed herbs
   such as thyme, marjoram, sage and rosemary
   mixed with a small amount of olive oil
   to help them stick together
4 cloves garlic, peeled but left whole
sea salt and freshly ground black pepper
1 shoulder of lamb, about 1.8kg (4lb) in weight,
   boned and rolled by your butcher –
   ask him not to roll it too tightly as you will be
   stuffing it with herbs
25g (1oz) butter
1 tablespoon olive oil
1 large onion, sliced
900g (2lb) whole new potatoes or halved old ones
450ml (16fl oz) hot meat stock made from the bones
   which your butcher has given to you

Preheat the oven to 170°C/325°F/Gas Mark 3. Press half the herbs, the garlic and seasoning inside the rolled lamb. Melt the butter and oil in a large, flameproof, ovenproof casserole dish and cook the onion until browned, stirring occasionally.

Add the lamb and cook until browned on all sides, turning frequently. Place the potatoes round the meat, then pour the stock over the meat. Cover with a tightly fitting lid and cook in the oven for about 2 hours, or until the lamb is cooked to your liking, adjusting the cooking time accordingly.

Before serving, adjust the seasoning and sprinkle with the remaining chopped herbs. Place the meat and potatoes on a warm serving dish, cover and keep hot. Boil the cooking juices over a high heat until reduced and then serve separately as an accompanying sauce.

LAMB STEW

I have adapted the traditional Irish Stew recipe by using olive oil instead of lard, which was the traditional fat. I have also added garlic which again is not in an Irish Stew but is used in its French equivalent *Carré d' Agneau Lorraine*.

SERVES 4-6

- 3 tablespoons olive oil
- 2 onions, sliced
- 4 leeks, washed and chopped
- 4 carrots, sliced
- 1 clove garlic, crushed
- sea salt and freshly ground black pepper
- 8 lamb cutlets from the best of neck, trimmed and partly boned by your butcher
- 1 bouquet garni, or bunch of fresh herbs tied with string
- 1.2 litres (2 pints) vegetable stock
- 8 potatoes, thickly sliced

Heat the oil in a heavy-based pan and fry the onions until soft, stirring occasionally. Add the leeks, carrots, garlic and seasoning and continue cooking until the vegetables start to take on colour, stirring occasionally.

Add the cutlets, brown slightly on either side and then add the bouquet garni and stock. Bring to the boil, then reduce the heat, cover and simmer on top of the stove for about 40 minutes, stirring occasionally.

Remove the pan from the heat, allow to cool and then skim off and discard the white skin of fat from the top of the stock. Add the sliced potatoes to the stew, adjust the seasoning and bring to the boil again. Simmer gently for about 10 minutes or until the potatoes are cooked and tender. Serve in large bowls with country bread (see page 22).

Opposite: The pigs sold through Graig Farm are raised slowly, taking about 20 weeks to reach maturity rather than the 12 weeks favoured by intensive farms.

PORK

Traditionally, a pig was central to family life and lived in close quarters with the family. In my Spanish village, the pig was often housed in a room next to the kitchen where it was ideally placed to finish all the peelings and left-overs. When I lived in Spain, once a year, the pig was butchered in an atmosphere of festivity. Neighbouring wives joined the hubbub as they gathered to help the madre (mother) collect the blood and clean the intestines ready to make sausages, black puddings and chorizo to carry them through the winter months. The men cut the animal into joints to sell or salt down for winter.

Personally, I like my pork simple and organic pork is so delicious that it is best to stick to the classic combinations – a tender pork fillet pan-fried with mushrooms and cream, a pork chop which has been marinated in honey and lemon juice and then gently roasted in the oven, or a juicy leg joint with crisp crackling and a tart apple sauce, served with traditional gravy and crunchy roast potatoes. And can anything beat the English favourite of traditional Bangers and Mash?

BANGERS & MASH WITH RED WINE AND ONION GRAVY

We use sausages from Longwood Farm made by Matthew and Louise Unwin from their organic field-reared pigs. The meadows where they browse are full of wild flowers and herbs and are alive with insects and butterflies in the summer. In autumn, the pigs are let loose into the orchard to eat the fallen apples and pears, so the meat is truly full of flavour.

Opposite:
Bangers & Mash with Red Wine and Onion Gravy

SERVES 4 (generous portions)

Allow at least 2 sausages per person

FOR THE RED WINE AND ONION GRAVY:

450g (1lb) onions, sliced

40g (1½oz) butter

40g (1½oz) brown sugar

300ml (½ pint) red wine

1 tablespoon balsamic vinegar

300ml (½ pint) vegetable stock
(this can be made up from Marigold vegetable stock powder and potato water)

1 tablespoon tomato purée (or more if you wish)

1 teaspoon chopped fresh or dried rosemary

sea salt and freshly ground black pepper

FOR THE MASH:

450g (1lb) potatoes, boiled in their skins

150ml (¼ pint milk)

55g (2oz) butter

sea salt and freshly ground black pepper

Prick the sausages to stop shrinkage and either fry or bake them until golden brown. Meanwhile put your potatoes on to boil (for maximum nutrition, keep the skins on – this is a more rough-and-ready mash but better for you! – and use the potato water for your stock to ensure you keep all the goodness in the dish).

Then prepare the gravy. Place the onions in a large saucepan with the butter and sugar and cook for about 10 minutes, until caramelized, stirring occasionally. Add the red wine and balsamic vinegar and turn up the heat to boil off the alcohol, then pour in the vegetable stock. Bring to the boil, then reduce the heat and simmer for about 15 minutes, stirring occasionally. Stir in the tomato purée, rosemary and seasoning to taste.

To make the mash, place the cooked potatoes in a saucepan with the milk, butter, salt and pepper. Heat gently and when the milk starts to simmer, remove the pan from the heat and mash with a hand masher or an electric mixer until smooth. Serve the cooked sausages alongside the mash with the gravy poured over the top.

FILLETS OF PORK
WITH PRUNES AND CREAM SAUCE

SERVES 4

450g (1lb) large prunes (about 20-24), soaked
425ml (¾ pint) white wine
approx. 700g (1lb 9oz) loin of pork,
   cut into 8 fillets of about 85g (3oz) each
seasoned plain flour, for coating
55g (2oz) butter
1 tablespoon redcurrant jelly or raspberry jam
250ml (9fl oz) double cream
sea salt and freshly ground black pepper

Place the prunes in an ovenproof dish, add half the wine and stir to mix, then leave to soak overnight.

Preheat the oven to 190°C/375°F/ Gas Mark 5. Bake the prunes and juices in the oven for 1 hour, then strain the prunes, reserving the prunes and juices separately. Set aside.

Coat the pork fillets all over with the seasoned flour. Melt the butter in a shallow pan and brown the meat gently on both sides, taking care that the butter does not burn. After about 10 minutes, pour in the remaining wine, cover the pan and cook very gently on top of the stove for about 45 minutes. Test the meat with a fork to see if it is tender.

Pour the reserved juice from the prunes over the meat, let it bubble for 5 minutes and then, using a slotted spoon, lift the meat into a warm, ovenproof serving dish. Place the prunes around the meat.

Opposite:
Barbecued Pork
served with rice.

Stir the redcurrant jelly or raspberry jam into the sauce in the pan, heating it gently, before adding the cream and seasoning. When the sauce is thick and shiny, pour it over the meat and prunes and serve immediately.

This dish is perfect on its own, just served with crusty bread and a green salad.

BARBECUED PORK

The first cooking I ever did in public was on an oil drum barbecue. We had seen them in South Africa and when we started a *Barbacoa* on the hillside above the village where we lived in southern Spain, we cooked on these. They are big oil drums, cut in half, with holes drilled into the bottom and legs added. The top was covered in a double layer of chicken wire. Big trunks from dead almond trees were gathered from the hillsides to fuel the fires and the resulting taste was fantastic.

You don't need to cook this on an oil drum, it will work in an ordinary barbecue or even in the oven!

SERVES 4

300ml (½ pint) apple juice
2 tablespoons brown sugar
1 tablespoon cider vinegar
1 tablespoon tamari
2 cloves garlic, crushed
1cm (½ in) piece of fresh root ginger, peeled and grated
4 large pork chops

To make the marinade, mix together the apple juice, sugar, vinegar, tamari, garlic and ginger in a bowl. Place the pork chops in a shallow, non-metallic dish and pour over the marinade. Turn the chops over in the marinade to coat them completely. Set aside and leave to marinate for at least 2 hours, then either barbecue or roast the chops in a preheated oven at 200°C/400°F/Gas Mark 6 for about 20-30 minutes or until cooked to your liking.

Serve the chops with their juices accompanied by rice or jacket potatoes cut open and a knob of garlic butter added.

in the wild

Before the days of intensive farming, game and wild (unfarmed) fish was rightly regarded as healthy, sustainable eating. Today, however, game, as well as sea and river fish, are almost certainly polluted to some degree by industrial and domestic waste. It seems totally ironic that we now need to farm our fish to be sure that they are not carrying harmful chemicals and we need to ensure that our game comes from organically-farmed estates which do not use pesticides. What hard work it is being a healthy food eater, I hear you sigh. Hopefully, it will become easier for us all as the demand for organic food grows.

ST HELENA'S
ORGANICALLY REGISTERED WILD FISH

St Helena is a tiny tropical island situated right in the centre of the South Atlantic, midway between southern Africa and South America. It is one of the most isolated communities in the world, being 1,125km away from Ascension Island and nearly 2,000km from the nearest continental landmass. It has no airport, and only one ship, the RMS *St Helena*, which journeys from the island to the UK just four or five times a year. Because of its isolation and the limited possiblities for travelling to and from the island, visitors are few. St Helena has a population of around 5,000 and relies heavily on fishing for its economic survival.

There is no industry on the island and the waters around the island are free from pollution. The fishing is carried out by around 50 fishermen and their system ensures that the process is fully sustainable. They use a fleet of small boats which travel only a few miles from the coast, leaving at dawn and returning in the afternoon of the same day. No large dragnets are used, only hook and line, which ensures that no dolphins are accidentally caught and killed.

The fresh catch is delivered each day to the small fish processor on the island which fillets, steaks, smokes and freezes fish for sale. The fact that the entire process is dealt with and controlled by the islanders themselves ensures the final product's high quality and also that the maximum income returns to the island.

St. Helena's organically registered wild fish may be bought from Graig Farm (see page 85, and contact details on page 177).

One of the small fleet of family-owned fishing boats based at St Helena. The boats leave for the day's fishing early in the morning, return in the evening and all the fish is processed the same day.

GAME

Game was far more commonly eaten before the days of intensive farming. A look through one of my favourite cookbooks, Elizabeth David's 'French Provincial Cooking', reveals no less than: four recipes for partridge, four for pheasant, one for plovers, one for woodcock, one for wild duck, one for teal, one for thrushes, one for pigeons, one for hare, two for venison and one for wild boar!

CANARD SAUVAGE A LA NAVARRAISE (WILD DUCK WITH SWEET PEPPER AND WHITE WINE)

I am going to include Elizabeth David's recipe for wild duck as this is the first one I ever cooked.

'From the giblets of a wild duck, plus carrot, onion, herbs, a glass of white wine, a spoonful of Madeira, a little water, and if possible, a piece of dried sweet red pepper – not the burning chilli pepper – make about ½ pint of stock, strain it and reduce by fast-boiling to ⅓ pint.

Prepare the following mixture: 2 shallots finely chopped, a carrot cut into small dice, ¼ lb gammon diced, half a fresh sweet pepper, all seeds and core removed, cut into little pieces. Melt this mixture in goose or pork fat or olive oil. When the shallots have taken colour put in the duck and let it gently brown. Warm a ladle of brandy, set light to it; pour it flaming over the duck. When the flames have died down, add the hot stock. Cover the pan, transfer to a medium oven at Gas No. 4, 355°F and cook for 35-40 minutes. Serve with its own sauce, triangles of fried bread and a green salad.'

In an old Canadian recipe book I found in an Ottawa second-hand book shop, there is a short instruction on wild duck which goes as follows:

'Before roasting, parboil with a small carrot, peeled and placed inside. This will absorb the fishy taste that is prevalent in most wild ducks. When parboiled (about 15 minutes), remove and discard the carrot. Lay the duck in fresh water for about half an hour then stuff with breadcrumbs, seasoned with salt and pepper, sage and a little chopped onion. Roast in a 350°C oven for about 1½ hours, basting frequently with drippings' (extract taken from a book entitled *Out of Old Nova Scotia Kitchens* by Mary Nightingale).

ROASTED WILD DUCK

Wild duck (Mallard) are usually served roasted – cooked fast in a fierce oven. You will also require a very sharp knife for jointing at speed. This is not a recipe for the squeamish or inexperienced cook!

SERVES 2
2 prepared wild duck, each about 900g (2lb)
115g (4oz) butter, softened
1 teaspoon allspice berries
sea salt and freshly ground black pepper
1 teaspoon freshly grated nutmeg
6 shallots or 1 onion, finely chopped
125ml (4fl oz) red wine

Preheat the oven to its highest possible setting – usually about 240°C/475°F/Gas Mark 9. Rub the ducks all over with half the butter and place them in a roasting tin. Roast in the oven for 8 to 10 minutes, then remove and place them on a board. With a sharp knife, remove the legs and wings. Pound the allspice berries with a little salt and the grated nutmeg and rub some of this mixture on the legs and wings.

Opposite: Wild Duck with Sweet Pepper and White Wine

Preheat the grill to high. Place the legs on a grill rack in a grill pan and grill them for a few minutes on either side until cooked and tender, then place them in a oven-proof dish and keep them warm at the bottom of the oven. Repeat this process with the wings.

Reduce the oven temperature to 200°C/400°F/Gas Mark 6. Lightly grease a separate ovenproof dish and sprinkle the dish with the shallots or onion. Carve the rest of the ducks into long thin fillets and place in the dish. Sprinkle the remaining allspice and nutmeg mixture onto the fillets, add the cooking juices from the roasting pan and the wine. Cover and cook in the oven for 20 minutes.

When ready to serve, place the fillets on a flameproof serving dish, then place two legs and two wings at each end of the serving dish. Distribute the remaining butter in dots over the fillets, then put the dish under a red hot grill for a minute or so for the top to glaze. Serve at once with mashed potatoes. This is delicious accompanied by an orange salad garnished with black olives.

PHEASANT WITH APPLES

This is a traditional Normandy recipe. It is very rich with lashings of cream and butter but you could substitute yoghurt for cream to make it lighter. Pheasant requires hanging for some days to develop its flavour. If you are hanging it yourself, you must hang it from the neck until the leading tail-feather can be plucked easily.

SERVES 4

225g (8oz) butter

2 young pheasants, each about 900g (2lb) in weight (if the biggest feather is pointed the bird is young, if it is rounded the bird is already old), prepared and oven-ready

8 medium-sized cooking apples

4 tablespoons brown sugar

850ml (1½ pints) double cream

sea salt and freshly ground black pepper

2 tablespoons roughly chopped fresh parsley

Preheat the oven to 200°C/400°F/Gas Mark 6. Melt half the butter in a sauté pan, add both pheasants and cook until brown on all sides, turning occasionally.

Meanwhile, peel and core the apples and chop them into small pieces. Melt the remaining butter in an earthenware casserole dish, add the apples and sugar and sauté until softened, stirring occasionally.

Place the pheasants on top of the apples with the juices from the sauté pan and pour the cream over the top. Place a lid on the casserole dish and cook in the oven for 25-30 minutes or until the pheasants are cooked and tender. Taste and adjust the seasoning, sprinkle over the parsley, then serve from the casserole.

This is delicious served with Fondant Potatoes (see recipe on page 80) and a cooked green vegetable such as spinach.

Opposite: Pheasant with Apples

GUINEA FOWL BRAISED IN RED WINE WITH SHALLOTS

The flavour of a guinea fowl is midway between that of a chicken and a pheasant. For two people allow one bird.

SERVES 4

- 115g (4oz) butter
- 2 oven-ready guinea fowl, each about 700-900g (1lb 9oz-2lb)
- 2 sprigs fresh thyme
- 450g (1lb) shallots
- 3 cloves garlic, finely chopped
- 2 tablespoons brown sugar
- 300ml (½ pint) red wine
- sea salt and freshly ground black pepper

Melt the butter in a heavy earthenware or iron dish on top of the stove, add the guinea fowl and cook until browned on all sides, turning once or twice.

Add the thyme and cook over a low heat for a further 20 minutes with the lid on, before adding the shallots and garlic. Cover and continue cooking for a further 15 minutes, or until the meat is cooked and the shallots are soft.

Take the fowl out of the pan, place on a board and carve. Place the carved meat on a warm serving dish, cover and keep warm.

Add the sugar to the shallots in the pan and cook, stirring, until the sugar is absorbed into the juices and the shallots become coated and start to caramelize. Remove the shallots from the pan and place them around the meat on the serving dish. Cover and keep warm.

Stir the red wine into the juices left in the pan, let it bubble and season to taste. Pour the sauce over the meat and shallots and serve. To make a richer dish, a little cream can be added to the sauce just before serving.

Again, I am going to recommend serving this dish with mashed potatoes because there is nothing like it with a rich sauce. This time, mash some cooked parsnips and carrots in with the potatoes.

WILD RABBIT IN MUSTARD SAUCE

Wild rabbits are pests that are responsible for immense damage to crops. If we eat more of them we would be doing something practical to protect our farmers' crops!

SERVES 4

FOR THE RABBIT:

- 115g (4oz) butter
- 2 tablespoons olive oil
- 1 onion, chopped
- 2 cloves garlic, crushed
- 2 wild rabbits, each about 700-900g (1lb 9oz-2lb), jointed and cleaned
- seasoned plain flour, for coating
- 1 bay leaf
- sea salt and freshly ground black pepper

FOR THE SAUCE:

- 55g (2oz) butter
- 25g (1oz) plain flour
- 1 tablespoon coarse grain mustard
- 2 teaspoons brown sugar
- 125ml (4fl oz) white wine
- 2 teaspoons stock powder (or sea salt and herbs)
- finely chopped fresh parsley, to garnish

For the rabbit, heat the butter and oil in a heavy-based saucepan and sauté the onions and garlic until soft and browning, stirring occasionally. Remove the onions and garlic from the pan and place on a plate. Roll the jointed rabbits in seasoned flour, add to the pan and cook until brown on all sides, turning occasionally.

Return the onion and garlic to the pan together with the bay leaf. Cover with water, add the seasoning, then

Opposite: Wild Rabbit in Mustard Sauce – deboned here by our Head Chef, Issa, to make a ballottine. It tastes just as good jointed, as described in the recipe but beware of the small bones. Write to us (see page 4) if you would like to know how to make a ballottine and we will send instructions.

bring to the boil, reduce the heat and allow to simmer, uncovered, for 30 minutes. When cooked, the rabbit should have the consistency of cooked chicken. Remove the rabbit from the pan, place on a plate, cover and keep it warm. Strain and reserve the rabbit stock.

Make the sauce: first make a paste by mixing the butter and flour together, heat this gently in a saucepan, then stir in the mustard, sugar, wine, stock powder and reserved rabbit stock. Heat gently, stirring continuously, until the sauce thickens.

Arrange the rabbit on a warm serving platter. Pour over the sauce and sprinkle with a generous amount of chopped parsley. Serve with plain boiled potatoes and glazed carrots which have been cooked with very little water, some butter and a sprinkling of sugar.

RABBIT FRICASSEE

SERVES 4

2 young rabbits, each about 700-900g (1lb 9oz-2lb)
sea salt
1 small onion, chopped
¼ teaspoon freshly ground black pepper
¼ teaspoon ground nutmeg
pinch of ground mace
1 tablespoon chopped fresh mixed herbs such as
    rosemary and thyme or 2 teaspoons dried mixed herbs
225ml (8fl oz) single cream or milk, plus a little extra
    milk for mixing with the flour
2 eggs, well-beaten
1 tablespoon butter
25g (1oz) plain flour
juice of 1 lemon

To prepare the rabbits, cut each one into joints and soak them in a bowl of salt water for at least 1 hour. Drain, place the rabbit joints in a pan and cover with fresh water. Add the onion, pepper, ground spices and herbs. Cover, bring to the boil, then reduce the heat and simmer for about 1 hour, until the rabbit is cooked and tender.

Remove the rabbit joints from the saucepan using a slotted spoon and place on a plate. Cover and keep warm in a low oven.

Strain the stock in which the rabbits were cooked and discard the contents of the sieve. Pour 450ml (16fl oz) of the stock into a pan, add the 225ml (8fl oz) cream or milk, fold in the beaten eggs a little at a time and add the butter. Mix the flour with a little extra milk and add to the pan. Bring slowly to the boil, stirring continuously, until the sauce thickens. Remove from the heat, stir in the lemon juice, then pour the sauce over the rabbits and serve hot with boiled rice.

WOOD PIGEON

Wood pigeons are one of our commonest birds – and taste delicious. Nowadays, they can be found in supermarkets and specialist butchers 'dressed and drawn'. The advantage of eating wood pigeon is that they are now reaching pest proportions, so we are not depleting any wild stocks, but rather helping the farmers to keep damaging bird pests at manageable levels.

I like them simply casseroled. So, select one young pigeon per person, brown them lightly in melted butter in a pan, then transfer them to a heavy earthenware dish ready for the oven. Into the butter in which the pigeons have browned, pour either two glasses (225ml/8fl oz) of red wine or, if you prefer a sweeter sauce, two glasses (225ml/8fl oz) of Madeira wine. A glass (125ml/4fl oz) of cognac gives a stronger flavour if you can run to it as well. Let this boil for a few seconds and then pour this over the birds.

Surround the birds with small onions, mushrooms and pieces of peeled, ripe tomatoes, all of which have been previously sautéed in butter. Add a further glass (125ml/4fl oz) of water or stock and season well with salt and pepper. Lard (cover) the breasts of the pigeons with bacon before cooking (the pigeon is a lean bird and will benefit from the larding).

Cover and cook in a preheated oven at 180°/350°F/ Gas Mark 4 for 50 minutes. Serve with mashed potatoes and, if you fancy it, 225ml (8fl oz) double cream stirred into the sauce just before serving.

VENISON STEW
WITH CRANBERRY SAUCE

Because venison is a lean meat, it tends to dry out easily and in France, venison is routinely marinated and then baked in a dough case for 4 to 5 hours. However, this is a long drawn-out process and I would favour a venison stew served with a fruit jelly or sauce.

Buy small pieces of venison already jointed and chopped for stewing – allow about 225-280g (8-10oz) venison per person. Rub the venison with a little ground allspice, sea salt and freshly ground black pepper, sauté in half butter and half olive oil in a pan until sealed all over.

Transfer to a flameproof, ovenproof casserole and pour two glasses (225ml/8fl oz) of red wine or port over the meat. Bring to the boil on top of the stove and boil rapidly for 1 minute, then add 850ml (1½ pints) of good hot stock. Bring to the boil once again and boil for about 5 minutes. Put the lid on and cook in a preheated oven at 170°C/325°F/Gas Mark 3 for 3 hours. Serve straight from the casserole with Cranberry Sauce (see below).

CRANBERRY SAUCE
SERVES 4
225g (8oz) fresh or frozen cranberries
finely grated rind and juice of 1 lemon
1 tablespoon brown sugar
55g (2oz) butter

Place the cranberries in a saucepan with sufficient water to moisten the bottom of the pan. Add the lemon rind and sugar. Simmer very slowly, uncovered, for about 20 minutes, until the fruit is soft, stirring all the time. Beat in the butter and add the lemon juice. Remove from the heat and allow to cool before serving.

The Cookshop team discussing the week's specials with Carol.

FISH

We go out of our way to support organic fish farming, because it protects our dwindling stocks of wild fish and avoids the chemical pollution and health hazards associated with conventional fish farming. Pollution of the seas and rivers by chemicals, sewage, heavy metals and other wastes damages the health of all wild fish, while over-fishing is a desperate problem which can only be solved by a reduction in consumption.

Normal fish farms invariably overstock and so need to use large amounts of pesticides and antibiotics (as in all intensive farming). By contrast, the organic fish farms are governed by a stringent set of rules, laid down by the Soil Association, which protects the health of the fish (and thus our own) and this is currently – in the view of most environmentalists – the only acceptable way to produce fish. The other option, of course, is simply not to eat fish at all!

Our sea fish are caught in the seas off St Helena – an island in the South Atlantic, half-way between South Africa and South America. We also buy farmed freshwater fish from two farms which use 'wild organic methods' in Northern Ireland and Northern Scotland. These are organically certified fish, but both these sources are expensive options. My next choice would be to buy fish frozen on the high seas in specially designed freezer ships. I saw for myself, on a Spanish fishing boat off Cape Town, the unpolluted waters they fish in and the speed with which the fish was processed and frozen on board.

Scallops are also now being intensively farmed, so make sure you specify 'free-range' ones. The scallops in this picture are wild and taste so wonderful that all you need to do is grill them, add a squeeze of lemon juice, and serve. You can taste the sea!

POACHED SALMON AND WATERCRESS SAUCE

Many people will not remember the days when salmon was a 'special occasion' fish, the expensive and sought-after creature it deserves to be. Intensive farming has changed all this and has also endangered the lives of salmon living in the wild. In the chapter entitled 'Why Eat Organic?' (page 168) you can read more about the problems of pesticide use in intensive fish farms. Suffice to say that when you can buy (or are given) a wild salmon, treat it with the respect it used to command, it deserves it.

SERVES 10-12

medium-sized salmon – approximately 2.7kg (6lb)

FOR THE COURT BOUILLON
450g (1lb) onions, roughly chopped
350g (12oz) carrots, roughly chopped
55g (2oz) coarse sea salt
300ml (½ pint) cider vinegar
bouquet garni or a sprig of fresh thyme and a bay leaf
15g (½oz) black peppercorns

Salmon is traditionally poached in a court bouillon or stock, which is prepared in the following way. Put all the ingredients, except the peppercorns, into a large pan with 5.7 litres (10 pints) water and bring to the boil. Simmer, uncovered, for 40 minutes, then add the peppercorns. Boil for a further 10 minutes, then remove from the heat and strain through a fine sieve into a bowl. Discard the contents of the sieve and set the stock aside to cool.

Lay the salmon – which you should get your fishmonger or fisherman to clean, wash and trim – in an appropriate pan (if you have a fish kettle this is perfect, but most people don't bother for such an occasional event). Cook the fish either whole or in cutlets already prepared for you.

Pour over the cooled stock and bring to the boil on top of the stove, then turn the heat down and cook with the lid on, without boiling, so that the fish is gently poached. Poach for about 15 minutes for a whole fish and about 6 minutes for a cutlet – the important thing is to keep the flesh from shrinking too rapidly and to keep the fish intact. Carefully remove the salmon from the hot stock, place on a plate and allow to cool. Serve warm or cold.

Alternatively, lots of people find it easier to cook whole salmon wrapped in foil, buttering the foil on the inside before wrapping it around the salmon. Use double foil so that it doesn't split and lose all the wonderful juices. Cook in a preheated oven at 180°C/350°F/Gas Mark 4 and allow roughly 1½ hours for a 900g (2lb) salmon, increasing the cooking time by 30 minutes for each extra 450g (1lb).

Serve the whole salmon or salmon cutlets either cold on a large serving dish accompanied by thinly sliced cucumbers which have been marinated in a mixture of cider vinegar and brown sugar and lashings of mayonnaise (see recipe on page 32) or serve warm with Watercress Sauce (see following recipe).

WATERCRESS SAUCE
SERVES 4
2 bunches watercress
25g (1oz) butter
1 onion, finely chopped
1 clove garlic, finely chopped
175ml (6fl oz) vegetable stock
300ml (½ pint) double cream
few drops of lemon juice
sea salt and freshly ground black pepper

Separate the leaves from the stalks of the watercress. Chop the leaves and set aside. Melt the butter in a pan and add the onion, garlic and watercress stalks. Cover and cook over a gentle heat for about 10 minutes, stirring

Opposite: Poached Salmon and Watercress Sauce

from time to time. Add the stock and bring to the boil, then reduce the heat and simmer for 5 minutes, stirring occasionally.

Strain the liquid, discarding the vegetables and return the liquid to the pan. Stir in the cream and watercress leaves and reheat gently until warm enough to serve. If preferred, the stock, cream and watercress leaves can be liquidized to make a smoother sauce, then reheated before serving. Stir in a few drops of lemon juice and add seasoning to taste.

TUNA NICOISE

There are many types of Niçoise salads – every chef has his or her own version – and this is because it was originally a seasonal salad with hard-boiled eggs, tomatoes, black olives and anchovy fillets as the only constants.

For a main course in the summer, we use fresh tuna on this salad: a Yellow Fin tuna which comes from St Helena (supplied by Graig Farm in Wales, see page 177), but you can substitute canned tuna. Make sure that the canners have a certificate from the Whale and Dolphin Society, however, which ensures that the tuna has been fished with a line and not caught with vast dragnets which endanger the lives of dolphins who get swept up in them and drown.

SERVES 4 FOR LUNCH

1 lettuce (preferably Cos which is crisp and
    flavourful)
115g (4oz) cooked firm potatoes (new potatoes
    are best), sliced
2 firm tomatoes, quartered
8 whole black olives
115g (4oz) cooked green beans
6 anchovy fillets
3 tablespoons cold-pressed olive oil
2 tablespoons cider vinegar
1 clove garlic, crushed
1 teaspoon mustard (any type will do)
sea salt and freshly ground black pepper
2 hard-boiled eggs, shelled and cut into quarters
1 tablespoon chopped fresh mixed herbs
    such as chives, chervil and tarragon
4 tuna steaks, each about 115g (4oz)
lemon juice, for sprinkling
sliced, deseeded red or green peppers,
    to garnish (optional)

Place the lettuce in a salad bowl, together with the potatoes, tomatoes, black olives, green beans and anchovies and toss to mix. In a separate bowl, mix the oil, vinegar, garlic, mustard and seasoning together and just before you are about to serve, pour this over the salad. Using salad servers or your hands, toss the salad and dressing together.

Arrange the salad on four plates, piling high in the centre and place the eggs around the sides. Sprinkle the fresh herbs over the salad. Sear the tuna steaks under a preheated hot grill or in a pan over a high heat, until cooked, turning once. Season with salt and pepper and a squeeze of lemon juice. Lay one tuna steak on top of each portion of salad and serve, garnished with sliced peppers, if liked.

Opposite: Tuna Niçoise

THREE TYPES OF FISHCAKE

For years, my husband and I have been on the look-out for the perfect fishcake. The jury is out on the following three, which we produce for the restaurant and the cookshops, having run a competition amongst the cooks!

LIZZIE'S SPICY FISHCAKES WITH TOMATO SAUCE

SERVES 4

450g (1lb) potatoes, peeled and diced
55g (2oz) butter
450g (1lb) cod fillet
sea salt and freshly ground black pepper
2 fresh green chillies, deseeded and finely chopped
2 cloves garlic, crushed
2 teaspoons grated fresh root ginger
2 tablespoons chopped fresh coriander
1 egg, beaten
dried breadcrumbs, for coating
sunflower oil, for frying

Cook the potatoes in a pan of boiling water until tender, then drain and mash them with the butter. Poach the cod in a pan of seasoned, simmering water for about 10 minutes, then drain and flake, taking care to remove and discard any rogue bones.

Combine the mashed potatoes, flaked cod, chillies, garlic, ginger, coriander and seasoning in a bowl (if the mixture is too dry bind it with a little beaten egg).

Shape into a roll on a floured board, then cut and make into 8 round cakes. Dip each round in the beaten egg, then coat with breadcrumbs. Heat a little oil in a large frying pan and fry the fishcakes until crisp and brown all over, turning once. Drain well and serve with the following quick, spicy tomato sauce.

Opposite: Lizzie's Spicy Fishcakes served with Tomato Sauce

TOMATO SAUCE

SERVES 4

225g (8oz) can organic chopped tomatoes
2 cloves garlic, crushed
1 small fresh red chilli, deseeded and chopped
juice of 1 lemon
1 tablespoon brown sugar
1 tablespoon chopped fresh coriander
1 tablespoon fresh torn basil leaves (optional)
sea salt and freshly ground black pepper, to taste

Put all the ingredients into a blender or food processor and chop roughly. Add torn basil leaves for a real taste of summer. Serve the cold tomato sauce with the hot fishcakes.

THOMAS'S SMOKED FISHCAKES

SERVES 4

450g (1lb) potatoes, boiled, drained and mashed
225g (8oz) smoked haddock, poached, boned and flaked
225g (8oz) cod fillet, poached, boned and flaked
finely grated rind of 1 lemon
2 tablespoons chopped fresh coriander
1 tablespoon fish sauce
2 teaspoons grated fresh root ginger
sea salt and freshly ground black pepper
1 egg, beaten
rolled cornflakes (see method below), for coating
sunflower oil, for frying

Make the fishcakes as before for Lizzie's Spicy Fishcakes, combining all the ingredients except the egg, cornflakes and oil, and shaping the mixture into 8 flat, round cakes, then dipping the fishcakes in beaten egg. Instead of rolling them in breadcrumbs try coating them in rolled cornflakes which you can make by putting the cornflakes in a clean plastic bag, tying a knot in the bag and rolling over them with a rolling pin. Cook the fishcakes in a little oil as above and serve hot with cold Green Herb Salsa (see page 122).

GREEN HERB SALSA

SERVES 4

20 capers

4 fresh anchovies (canned will do)

1 clove garlic, crushed

1 tablespoon chopped fresh coriander

1 tablespoon olive oil

Finely chop the capers and anchovies. Place them in a bowl with the garlic, coriander and oil and mix well. You can also blend these ingredients together but it loses a lot of texture.

SIMON'S SALMON FISHCAKES

SERVES 4

450g (1lb) potatoes, boiled, drained and mashed

450g (1lb) fresh salmon, poached, boned and flaked

2 teaspoons Dijon mustard

finely grated rind and juice of 1 lemon

1 tablespoon finely chopped fresh parsley

1 tablespoon finely chopped fresh chives

1 egg, beaten

dried breadcrumbs, for coating

sunflower oil, for frying

Make the fishcakes as before for Lizzie's Spicy Fishcakes, combining all the ingredients, except the egg, breadcrumbs and oil, shaping the mixture into 8 flat, round cakes, dipping the fishcakes in beaten egg and then coating them with breadcrumbs. Cook the fishcakes in a little oil as above and serve hot. These fishcakes are lovely with the watercress sauce that we give for the poached salmon (see page 116), but either of the above sauces are also good.

This substantial herb stuffing makes an excellent textural contrast with the delicate flesh of the fish.

STUFFED CARP
SERVED WITH NOODLES

English freshwater fish such as carp and pike used to be popular for celebrations, and still are in Eastern Europe. Of course, they are only as organic as the water in which they were caught.

SERVES 4

one thick slice white or wholemeal bread, about 115g (4oz), cut into cubes

350ml (12fl oz) dry white wine

3 tablespoons butter

1 onion, chopped

2 shallots, finely chopped

1 clove garlic, crushed

12 boiled and peeled fresh or canned chestnuts, chopped

1 tablespoon chopped fresh parsley

1 teaspoon salt

¼ teaspoon each of ground mace, ground bay leaves, dried thyme and freshly ground black pepper

1 egg, beaten

1.3kg (3lb) carp

Stuff the fish fairly liberally because it will be held in place by the trussing.

Preheat the oven to 190°C/375°F/Gas Mark 5. Soak the bread in 125ml (4fl oz) wine in a bowl, then squeeze the bread dry, reserving the wine and bread separately. Set aside. Melt the butter in a pan, add the onions and shallots and cook gently until soft, stirring occasionally.

Add the reserved bread and all the remaining ingredients except the remaining wine, egg and carp and mix well. Remove from the heat and allow to cool, before adding the egg to bind.

Stuff the cavity and head of the carp with this mixture. It is a good idea to truss the carp so that the stuffing does not escape. Place the stuffed fish in an earthenware ovenproof dish, then pour over the remaining wine and the reserved wine that the bread was soaked in.

Bake in the oven, uncovered, for 30 minutes, until the fish is cooked. Serve with home-made noodles (see nouilles recipe on page 42) and a lightly boiled or steamed green vegetable such as broccoli.

PIKE WITH WHITE BUTTER SAUCE

In France, pike is a speciality of the Loire region and is traditionally accompanied by a *beurre blanc* (white butter sauce), but this fish is prevalent throughout the fresh water lakes and coarse fishing rivers of the UK. In the absence of pike try other white fish. Even the once despised whiting makes a perfectly good – if inferior – replacement.

SERVES 4

  1 medium-sized pike, about 1.3kg (3lb)
  OR 1 whiting per person
  300ml (½ pint) white wine
  3 shallots
  3 tablespoons cider vinegar
  175g (6oz) butter

Poach your chosen, prepared fish in the simmering white wine in a pan until cooked – about 20 minutes depending on the size of the fish – the fish is cooked when you can ease the flesh away from the bones easily. Remove the fish using a slotted spoon, place on a plate, cover and keep warm in a low oven. Strain and reserve 3 tablespoons of the cooking juices.

WHITE BUTTER SAUCE

Chop the shallots very finely and put them in a small saucepan with the vinegar and reserved cooking juices, then cook until the shallots are completely soft and there is practically no liquid left in the saucepan, stirring occasionally. Remove from the heat and allow the mixture to cool.

  Return to a gentle heat, then gradually add the butter, about 25g (1oz) at a time, whisking continuously. As the butter softens, remove from the heat as the butter should never melt. The consistency of the sauce should be that of thick cream. This sounds easy to make, but it does take practice as the temperature of the butter is all important.

Before serving, strip the skin from the cooked pike and lift the flesh off the bones, making sure that you remove all the sharp, spiky ones. Beware, because pike has javelin-like bones between each muscle in the flesh and there are a lot of them – so warn your guests.

Serve the pike with the sauce spooned over it and crisp sautéed potatoes to which a large handful of chopped parsley has been added to the pan at the last minute.

MOULES A LA CREME

Dieppe springs to mind whenever Moules à la Crème is mentioned. For at least three decades after the war, to cross from England to France was to cross from a gastronomic desert to a gastronomic oasis and this dish was the first of many wonderful meals on the French shore.

SERVES 4

  2kg (4lb 8oz) fresh mussels in shell
  1 onion, finely chopped
  sea salt and freshly ground black pepper
  350ml (12fl oz) white wine
  300ml (½ pint) single cream
  finely chopped fresh parsley, to garnish

Fill the sink with salted water and scrub the mussels thoroughly, cutting off any 'beards' and rough bits.

  Toss the mussels into a wok heated over a high heat, add the onions, salt and pepper, and as the mussels start to open, pour in the wine, toss together and then add the single cream, tossing to mix.

  When all the mussels are open – this should take about 5 minutes – serve in large bowls and garnish with chopped parsley. Serve with thick slices of fresh country bread.

Opposite: Moules à la Crème

sweet things

The great thing about organic puddings is you can almost convince yourself that they are good for you!. By using unprocessed, organic ingredients, the range and richness of flavours come powerfully into focus. Raw unrefined sugar, for instance, gives a very different taste to white refined sugar, while the chocolate we use has a much higher content of cocoa solids than most chocolates, and this is reflected in the richness of the puddings. Organically grown fruit can be a taste revelation compared to the watery, pappy supermarket equivalents that go by the same name.

The dried fruit we use has not only been organically grown but also dried naturally. It has been sprayed neither with sulphur to preserve it, nor mixed with flavourings – including sugar and salt – in the way that many conventionally dried fruit products are.

You will certainly notice the difference when eating organic apples which have been grown without pesticides, picked when ripe – in the right season – and stored for shorter periods of time, without the use of post-harvest sprays. Conventional apples are sprayed with up to 20 different types of pesticides – so avoid them!

GREEN AND BLACK

For our first two recipes, we use Green and Black's chocolate – a company which describes itself as 'people and planet friendly'. Its chocolate is organic, fair-traded and top quality too, containing a rich 70% cocoa solids content.

Cocoa beans are more heavily sprayed with pesticides than any other food crop. Green and Black growers are not allowed to spray with fungicides and insecticides, however, so that not only is the chocolate pesticide-free, but the farmers are also protected from the sprays which play havoc with their own health world-wide.

Green and Black growers belong to farming co-operatives who sell the cocoa beans direct for a fair price, rather than through middle men who can manipulate the market leaving the growers with a pittance.

The chocolate is carefully made, too. Instead of the crude modern milling and processing techniques, Green and Black chocolate is blended by traditional methods and stirred for several days, to ensure optimum flavour and smoothness.

Jo Fairley, the founder of Green and Black, with Miguel Mis on a small family-owned cocoa grove in Belize, Central America.

CHOCOLATE AND ALMOND CAKE

This is a rich and luxurious dark chocolate cake. It is wheat-free, too, and will serve just as easily as a pudding.

SERVES 8

FOR THE CAKE:

115g (4oz) butter, softened

115g (4oz) brown sugar

150g (5½ oz) or 1½ bars dark chocolate
   (we use Green and Black's), broken into squares

140g (5oz) ground almonds

5 eggs, separated

FOR THE ICING:

55g (2oz) butter

50g (1¾ oz) dark chocolate, broken into squares

25g (1oz) flaked almonds

Grease a deep 20cm (8in) round cake tin and set aside. Preheat the oven to 190°C/375°F/Gas Mark 5. Make the cake. In a bowl, beat the butter and sugar together, by hand, or in a food processor. Melt the chocolate in a bowl placed over a pan of boiling water or in a bain marie.

In a large bowl, mix together the melted chocolate and ground almonds, then add the creamed butter and sugar

**Opposite:
Chocolate and
Almond Cake**

and stir together to mix. Mix the egg yolks into the chocolate mixture.

In a separate bowl, whisk the egg whites until stiff, then fold them into the chocolate mixture with a metal spoon. Transfer to the prepared cake tin and level the surface.

Bake in the oven for 40 minutes or until a skewer or sharp knife inserted into the centre comes out clean. Turn out and cool on a wire rack.

Make the icing by melting the butter with the chocolate in a bowl over a pan of boiling water. The butter gives it a lovely shiny look. Stir the chocolate and butter together and spread over the cake, then scatter the almonds over the top and serve in slices.

CHOCOLATE BROWNIES

MAKES 8 SQUARES

125g (4½oz) plain chocolate, broken into squares

175g (6oz) butter

4 eggs

140g (5oz) brown sugar

1½ teaspoons pure vanilla extract

350g (12oz) self-raising flour, sifted
   (you can use half flour and half ground almonds
   to make these brownies more luxurious still!)

Grease and line a 20cm (8in) square cake tin. Preheat the oven to 180°C/350°F/Gas Mark 4. Melt the chocolate and butter together in a bowl over a saucepan of simmering water.

In a separate bowl, whisk the eggs and sugar together until thick, pale and creamy – this will take about 5 minutes using a mixer. Stir in the melted chocolate and butter and vanilla extract, then fold in the flour (or flour and ground almonds).

Pour the mixture into the prepared tin. Bake in the oven for about 30 minutes or until slightly firm at the edges. Leave to cool in the tin, then cut into squares, remove from the tin and serve.

UPSIDE-DOWN APPLE AND FUDGE CAKE

SERVES 8

FOR THE CAKE:

2 medium-sized cooking apples

175g (6oz) brown sugar

115g (4oz) butter, softened

3 eggs

115g (4oz) self-raising flour

1 teaspoon baking powder

FOR THE FUDGE ICING:

115g (4oz) butter

115g (4oz) brown sugar

2 tablespoons double cream

Grease a 20cm (8in) round cake tin (a springform tin is best) and set aside. Preheat the oven to 190°C/375°F/Gas Mark 5. To make the cake, peel, core and slice the apples and lay them over the bottom of the tin. Sprinkle with 55g (2oz) sugar and set aside.

In a bowl, beat the butter and remaining 115g (4oz) sugar together until creamy. Beat in the eggs, then sift the flour and baking powder into the creamed mixture and fold in using a metal spoon. Lift your spoon high to introduce air into the mixture as you stir. Spoon this mixture over the apples, covering them completely.

Bake in the oven for about 30 minutes or until a skewer or sharp knife inserted into the centre comes out clean. Turn out and cool on a wire rack.

To make the fudge icing, melt the butter and sugar in a small saucepan until they turn a golden brown colour, stirring. Remove from the heat, stir in the double cream, then return the pan to the heat for a few seconds, stirring, until the mixture becomes a golden fudge.

Spread this fudge icing evenly over the apples. This cake is delicious eaten hot or cold and served in slices.

Right: Caramelized Orange Cheesecake
Opposite: Upside-down Apple and Fudge Cake

ORANGE CHEESECAKE

Our cake chef Anne invented the caramelized oranges for this cheesecake to use up an abundance of oranges.

SERVES 6-8

FOR THE CHEESECAKE:

200g (7oz) digestive biscuits

115g (4oz) butter, melted

6 eggs

140g (5oz) brown sugar

250g (9oz) mascarpone cheese

200g (7oz) creme fraiche

300g (10½ oz) natural yoghurt

finely grated zest of 2 lemons

2 drops of vanilla extract

FOR THE CARAMELIZED ORANGES:

2 medium oranges

115g (4oz) brown sugar

chocolate flakes, to garnish

Opposite:
Lemon Tart

LEMON TART

This is Issa's classic lemon tart and we glaze it with a blow torch, but don't try this at home.

SERVES 8

FOR THE SWEET PASTRY:

115g (4oz) plain flour

25g (1oz) icing sugar, sifted

85g (3oz) butter, cut into small cubes

1 egg

½ tablespoon milk

FOR THE FILLING:

finely grated zest and juice of 3 lemons

85g (3oz) icing sugar, sifted

3 eggs

300ml (½ pint) double cream

Start by preparing the caramelized oranges. Place the whole oranges in a pan with 600ml (1 pint) water, bring to the boil, then reduce the heat and simmer, uncovered, for about 1 hour, or slightly longer if the fruit is not quite softened. Remove from the heat and strain the oranges, reserving the oranges and cooking juices separately (there should be about 2 tablespoons of cooking juices left). Cool slightly, then chop the oranges into small pieces, removing and discarding the seeds, but taking care to retain any juice.

Return the chopped oranges and their juice, plus the reserved cooking juices to the saucepan with the sugar. Cook over a low heat for about 45 minutes, until caramelized, stirring occasionally. Set aside to cool.

Make the cheesecake. Grease a 23cm (9in) square cake tin. Preheat the oven to 180°C/350°F/Gas Mark 4. Tie the digestive biscuits up in a clean plastic carrier bag or freezer bag and crush them using a rolling pin, then place in a bowl and mix in the melted butter. Press the biscuit mixture evenly over the base of the tin.

In a large bowl, whisk the eggs and sugar together until thick, pale and creamy, then gradually stir in the mascarpone, creme fraiche and yoghurt. Add the lemon zest and vanilla extract and mix well. Pour over the biscuit base and bake in the oven for 45 minutes until lightly set.

Leave to cool in the tin, then turn out carefully onto a serving plate and spread the orange mixture over the top. Chill, garnish with chocolate flakes and serve.

Lightly grease a 23cm (9in) round tart tin. Preheat the oven to 220°C/425°F/Gas Mark 7. First make the pastry. Mix together the flour and icing sugar in a food processor and with the motor running, slowly introduce the butter cubes (alternatively, mix the flour and icing sugar in a bowl and rub in the butter). Add the egg and milk and mix to form a dough, then roll the dough into a ball, wrap in a clean dampened tea towel and chill in the refrigerator for 20 minutes.

Roll the pastry out on a lightly floured surface and line the tin. Chill in the refrigerator for 10 minutes. Cover with greaseproof paper and fill with baking beans, bake in the oven for 7 minutes, then remove the baking beans and greaseproof paper and bake for a further 5 minutes.

Meanwhile make the filling. Place the lemon zest and juice in a large bowl or a food processor. Add the icing sugar and eggs and beat together by hand, or blend for just 30 seconds, then add the cream and mix well or blend briefly to mix. Reduce the oven temperature to 180°C/350°F/Gas Mark 4. Pour the lemon mixture into the pastry case, then bake for a further 15 minutes until set. Serve warm or cold in slices.

SEASONAL FRUIT CRUMBLE

This is a seasonal crumble, so you can adapt the recipe to use whatever fruit is available – apple, pear, plum, rhubarb, currants are all suitable. If you are short of fruit or want a change try adding dried fruit. Here we have added some dried cranberries to give an extra tangy taste.

SERVES 4

FOR THE FRUIT BASE:

900g (2lb) seasonal fresh fruit, cut into pieces
(peeled and cored where necessary)

2 tablespoons dried cranberries

55-85g (2-3oz) brown sugar (this depends on the fruit
you are using, so you will need to add sugar to taste)

FOR THE CRUMBLE:

150g (5½oz) plain flour

100g (3½oz) butter

75g (2¾oz) brown sugar

Preheat the oven to 200°C/400°F/Gas Mark 6. Place the prepared fresh fruit and dried cranberries in a large, shallow ovenproof dish and sprinkle sugar to taste over the top.

To make the crumble, either whizz all the ingredients together in a food processor for a few seconds until the mixture resembles breadcrumbs, or place the flour in a bowl, rub in the butter, then stir in the sugar. Sprinkle about 1 tablespoon of water over the crumble, stirring with a fork, then scatter the crumble over the fruit.

Bake in the oven for about 35 minutes, until crisp and golden on top. The juices from the fruit will bubble through the crumble crust. Serve with cream or Proper Custard (see page 136).

A variation on this pudding is made by my mother-in-law, Olwen Jones, who uses fresh rhubarb, finely grated zest and juice of an orange and 1 teaspoon ground ginger, for the fruit base.

Opposite: Seasonal Fruit Crumble

TRADITIONAL SHERRY TRIFLE

SERVES 4-6

FOR THE SPONGE:

2 eggs

55g (2oz) caster sugar (we grind our brown
granulated sugar)

85g (3oz) plain flour

FOR THE TRIFLE:

raspberry or strawberry jam, for spreading

150ml (¼ pint) medium sherry

55g (2oz) flaked almonds

425ml (¾ pint) Proper Custard (see page 136),
cooled slightly but still warm (when cooling the
custard, stir occasionally to prevent a skin forming
on the top)

300ml (½ pint) double cream

flaked almonds, crystallized violets and angelica,
to decorate (optional)

Grease and flour a 20cm (8in) sandwich cake tin and set aside. Preheat the oven to 190°C/375°F/Gas Mark 5. Make the sponge. Whisk the eggs and sugar together in a large bowl until thick, pale and creamy, then sift the flour over the mixture and fold in gently.

Pour the mixture into the prepared tin and bake in the oven for 20-25 minutes, until risen, golden and the sponge springs back when pressed. Turn out and cool on a wire rack.

When cool, cut the sponge cake in half horizontally, spread the cut surface of the bottom half with jam and replace the other cake half on top. Cut the whole cake into small pieces and place in a shallow glass serving bowl. Pour the sherry over the cake and leave to soak for 30 minutes.

Sprinkle the flaked almonds over the cake, then pour the still warm custard over the almonds. Cover with a damp cloth or clingfilm and chill for about 2 hours.

Whip the cream in a bowl until stiff peaks form, then spread or pipe the cream over the custard. If you want a

traditional look, use a piping bag and nozzle to do fancy rosettes. Decorate with flaked almonds, crystallized violets and angelica.

PROPER CUSTARD

Proper custard is almost as easy to make as instant and an extremely versatile accompaniment to many puddings.

MAKES 600ml (1 pint)
    500ml (18fl oz) milk
    1 vanilla pod or ½ teaspoon pure vanilla extract
    6 egg yolks
    75g (2¾oz) brown sugar

Heat the milk and vanilla together in a saucepan and slowly bring to the boil. If you are using a vanilla pod, split it open before heating as it is the seeds which will flavour the milk. Just before the milk comes to the boil, remove the pan from the heat and leave to stand for 20 minutes. Remove and discard the vanilla pod, if using.

In a bowl, whisk the egg yolks and sugar together until thick, then pour the milk over them. Return the mixture to a clean saucepan and stir continuously over a low heat, until the mixture resembles double cream, taking care not to allow the mixture to boil.

TIPSY OATS

This is adapted from the Scottish *Cranachan*. We make it with our own curd cheese (see recipe on page 152), but you can use mascarpone cheese instead.

SERVES 4-6
    125g (4½oz) porridge oats
    75g (2¾oz) brown sugar
    250g (9oz) curd cheese or mascarpone cheese
    3 tablespoons whisky or brandy, plus extra for drizzling
    300ml (½ pint) double cream, lightly whipped
    250g (9oz) fresh soft fruit, such as raspberries or
        strawberries

Place the oats and sugar in a pan and cook over a high heat for 3-4 minutes, stirring every 30 seconds, until toasted. Remove from the heat and set aside to cool.

Place the curd cheese or mascarpone in a bowl, add 3 tablespoons of whisky or brandy and beat until smooth and well mixed. Fold in the cream and the cooled oat mixture, then fold in the fruit, taking care not to break up the fruit.

Spoon into glass serving bowls and drizzle a little extra whisky or brandy on top of each serving. Serve at once or chill before serving.

**Left: Home-made Curd Cheese (see page 152)
Opposite: Tipsy Oats**

Opposite:
Pashka is turned
out of its flow-
erpot and
served in slices.

PASHKA

The Russian version of curd cheese pudding is Pashka. When my daughter, Harriet, was studying in St Petersburg she was invited to eat this traditional Russian Easter dish and loved it. The closest pudding to her description is from Rose Elliot's excellent book *The Supreme Vegetarian Cookbook*. In Russia they use a Pashka mould made from wood, but you can use a clay flower pot, scrubbed and baked in a hot oven (about 220°C/425°F/Gas Mark 7) for 30 minutes, or a 1kg (2lb 4oz) yoghurt pot with some holes pierced in the bottom.

SERVES 6

2 egg yolks

85g (3oz) brown sugar

few drops of vanilla extract

4 tablespoons single cream

115g (4oz) unsalted butter, softened

700g (1lb 9oz) curd cheese

55g (2oz) candied peel, chopped

55g (2oz) blanched almonds, chopped

In a bowl, beat the egg yolks, sugar and vanilla extract together until pale and foamy. Heat the cream in a pan to just below boiling point, then pour onto the egg yolk mixture, stirring well.

Return the mixture to the saucepan and heat gently, stirring continuously, until thickened, being careful not to let the mixture boil or it will curdle. Remove from the heat and set aside.

Beat the butter in a bowl until light and creamy, then gradually add the egg mixture, stirring all the time. Continue stirring briskly and add the curd cheese, little by little. Finally, add the candied peel and almonds, mixing well.

Cut out a base and sides from greaseproof paper to fit your chosen pot. Line the flower pot or yoghurt pot with the greaseproof paper and spoon in the cheese mixture. Fold the ends of the kitchen paper over the top. Place a plate on top with a weight on it. Stand the pot on a plate to catch any moisture that seeps out of the base and refrigerate for 6 to 8 hours or overnight. Turn out onto a serving plate and serve in slices.

STICKY TOFFEE PUDDING

Our restaurant is located in a London mews and during the long, dark days of winter, when the weather is cold and wet, people need a special incentive to bring them out of their warm homes. This recipe is it – it was passed on to me by my step-son, Matthew, who lives in the Lake District, where it was apparently invented.

SERVES 8

FOR THE PUDDING:

115g (4oz) butter, softened

175g (6oz) brown sugar

3 eggs, beaten

225g (8oz) self-raising flour

300ml (½ pint) strong black coffee

1 teaspoon vanilla extract

225g (8oz) stoned dates, chopped

1 teaspoon bicarbonate of soda

FOR THE TOFFEE SAUCE:

85g (3oz) brown sugar

55g (2oz) butter

3 tablespoons double cream

Grease a deep 23cm (9in) round cake tin and set aside. Preheat the oven to 180°C/350°F/Gas Mark 4. Make the pudding. Cream the butter and sugar together in a bowl, then gradually beat in the eggs.

Sift the flour and fold it into the creamed mixture, then stir in the coffee, vanilla extract, dates and bicarbonate of soda. Turn into the prepared tin and bake for 1½ hours.

Make the toffee sauce. Place the sugar, butter and cream in a pan and heat gently until melted, stirring. Turn the hot cooked pudding out onto a flameproof serving plate and pour the toffee sauce over the top. Place under a preheated hot grill for a few minutes until the toffee sauce starts to bubble. Serve hot with extra double cream, if liked.

BREAD AND BUTTER PUDDING

This is a very under-rated dish, not least because it is a wonderful way of using up left-over bread, croissants and brioche. We have added the zest and juice of a lemon to this recipe to give it an extra zing!

Opposite: Sticky Toffee Pudding
Below: Bread and Butter Pudding

SERVES 4-6

55g (2oz) butter, softened

3 large slices of white bread
   or 6 croissant or brioche, sliced thinly

3 tablespoons sultanas

55g (2oz) flaked almonds

300ml (½ pint) milk

300ml (½ pint) single cream

1 tablespoon brown sugar

1 teaspoon ground cinnamon

2 egg yolks

finely grated zest and juice of 1 lemon

Grease a 24 x 24cm (9½ x 9½in) square cake tin and set aside. Spread the butter over the sliced bread, croissant or brioche on both sides. Cut into small triangles. Sprinkle the sultanas over the bottom of the prepared tin, then fill the tin with rows of overlapping bread triangles.

Sprinkle the flaked almonds over the top. Warm the milk and cream together in a saucepan, then stir in the sugar and cinnamon. Remove from the heat and beat the egg yolks together before stirring them into the milk mixture with the lemon zest and juice.

Right: Fruit Jam straight from the freezer (see page 158). Opposite: Scones and Cream

Pour this over the bread and leave to stand for 30 minutes to allow the bread to absorb the liquid. Preheat the oven to 180°C/350°F/Gas Mark 4. Bake the bread pudding in the oven for about 30 minutes until the top is browned. Serve warm or cold.

SCONES AND CREAM

Our cake chef Anne is also our Queen of Scones! No-one can make perfect, fluffy scones quite like her. When she brings a trayful out of the kitchen, they are gone before she can get back to the oven for more! Be sure to preheat the oven and prepare the baking sheet before mixing the dough, as scones must be cooked immediately after preparation.

MAKES 10 SCONES

225g (8oz) self-raising flour

½ teaspoon salt

1 teaspoon baking powder

55g (2oz) butter, cut into small squares

150ml (¼ pint) milk

115g (4oz) sultanas (optional)

fresh whipped cream and red fruit jam, to serve

Lightly flour a baking sheet and set aside. Preheat the oven to 230°C/450°F/Gas Mark 8. Sift the flour, salt and baking powder into a large bowl, then lightly rub in the butter until it resembles fine breadcrumbs. Make a well in the centre, pour in the milk, then stir the dry ingredients including the sultanas, if using, into the milk, in a circular fashion, to make a soft dough.

Turn out the dough onto a floured surface and knead quickly and lightly. Roll out the dough, either with a rolling pin or with the heel of your hand, until it is about 2cm (¾in) thick. Cut into rounds with a 5cm (2in) cutter.

Place on the prepared baking sheet and bake in the oven for 8-10 minutes, until well-risen and golden brown. Transfer to a wire rack to cool.

Serve warm, split and filled with whipped cream and red fruit jam. Try the recipe for Freezer Jam on page 158.

Preserving – a way of life

Preserving was vital before the days of refrigeration because it ensured an all-year-round supply of food. So, when there were seasonal gluts of fruit and vegetables, or fish and game were in season, this was all preserved for future use. Many varied techniques were devised to preserve food and prevent it from spoiling but as commercial food processing became more sophisticated, the need to conserve our own home-grown produce became less important. Now, if you want to make the most of the organic harvest from each season, preserving becomes important once more! Of course, the home freezer is one of the simplest and most convenient means of home preserving but there are many more that are fun to do and apply to a whole range of ingredients

In northern Europe, smoking was a favoured method for preserving meat and fish. In southern Europe, vegetables and fruit were sun-dried and fish was conserved in salt from the sea it was fished from. Today, these traditional ways of conserving food are still used giving us smoked fish, cured ham or sun-dried tomatoes. Pickles, jams and candied fruits can all be made using old-fashioned methods and the taste rewards are great. Although the freezer has the edge over salting runner beans these days, many of the natural ways to preserve are as effective as ever. As well as drying and smoking you can preserve fresh ingredients in sugar (the Romans used honey), vinegar, alcohol, oils, and other fats. All of these have the same purpose: to prevent the growth of yeasts, moulds and bacteria which cause the food to spoil. This is why the sterilization of jars is so important.

Always use sterilized containers with the appropriate lids and seals. You will also need vinegar-proof lids for chutneys and pickles, and waxed paper discs and cellophane seals for jams and other sweet preserves. All the equipment is available from good kitchen suppliers.

To sterilize your jars and bottles, you can either:

a) Submerge them in boiling water for 10 minutes, drain on a clean cloth, dry off in a cool oven and then fill with the hot product. Immerse all rubber rings, lids and corks in boiling water for 1 minute, then drain, dry and use as required.

OR

b) Place the clean jars on a baking sheet in a preheated oven at 170°C/325°F/Gas Mark 3 for 10 minutes. Allow them to cool slightly, and then fill with the hot product.

Examine pre-serving jars carefully before use as any cracks or chips around the rim may prevent the lid from sealing properly.

DRYING

Dried fruit and vegetables have a very long shelf-life. When dried, you can store them either in olive oil or exactly as they are, rehydrating them by soaking them in hot water. If you live in a warm climate, you can dry produce outdoors under the rays of the sun. Otherwise, it works perfectly well in a slow oven, which is the method we use at the Organic Café. Another option is to air-dry produce by stringing the harvest up in an airy room.

In France, I remember going mushroom picking in the forests each autumn. We would thread the mushrooms on a piece of string with a knot at the bottom and hang them in the loft to dry. When I lived in Spain, we had no mushrooms but lots of chillies and these were also dried on strings which decorated our porch all year round.

Produce that we don't dry ourselves, comes from a company called *Tropical Wholefoods*. This is exactly the sort of company we like to do business with. It is not only organic, but also a 'fair trade company', which means that it benefits the environment and safeguards our health, as well as protecting the small farmers who produce the goods by paying them directly.

Tropical Wholefoods was set up by Adam Brett in the 1980s. Its origins are in Uganda, where he grew up. He left during the Idi Amin era in the l970s, but went back in the 1980s as peace returned. What he found was a country devastated by years of civil war and despotism – but a country, too, whose rich, fertile soils could still produce abundant, high-quality fruits.

Adam saw that a low cost way of processing these fruits was needed in order to bring direct benefits to the small farmers. Since there were no canning factories, nor any glass manufacturers, the only chance was to preserve these fruits in the hot African sun. Sun-dried fruit was the answer! Working with two Ugandan partners, a wooden solar dryer was devised – nicknamed the 'Miracle Dryer' by the Ugandan press. Now over 100 different farmers own these solar dryers, which they use to produce a whole range of dried foods including mangoes, papayas, pineapples, bananas, tomatoes and oyster mushrooms.

It's fun to dry your own food though – under the sun, or in a warm oven – and it is a great way to use up over-ripe tomatoes. Drying can be used to preserve all kinds of fruit (simply halved or sliced and then oven-dried) and vegetables (halved or sliced, then sprinkled with salt and herbs as described on following page), but it really works well for tomatoes.

BOUQUET GARNI Buy 1 or 2 metres (yards) of muslin and cut into squares approximately 10cm (4in) in size. Fill each square with sprigs of fresh rosemary and thyme, a bay leaf and 12 black peppercorns and tie each one up into a bundle with string. Use in stews and casseroles to add delicious flavour. Store in an airtight jar for up to 2 months.

Left: The solar dryer dubbed 'The Miracle Dryer' is used by Ugandan farmers to dry fruit and vegetables like the chilli peppers opposite.

OVEN-DRIED TOMATOES

I do not really understand why oven-dried organic tomatoes taste so wonderful, but they do. The flavour is intensified in the slow baking and the joy is that they can be preserved in oil to eat all year round.

Because organic tomatoes are expensive at the best of times, we dry and preserve kilos of them when the prices are low at the peak of the harvest.

Wipe the tomatoes and cut them in half. Place cut side up on a wire mesh rack (the sort used for cooling cakes) and place this on a baking tray. Sprinkle with coarse sea salt and chopped fresh thyme – add rosemary, too, if you like this strong herb flavour.

Set the oven at 110°C/225°F/Gas mark ¼, and, leaving the oven door slightly open to allow the humidity to escape during the drying process, place the tomatoes in the oven and leave for about 8 hours (overnight is good, as long as you don't forget that they are in there!) The tomatoes should be dry, but not dried out, and slightly chewy but still soft. They should definitely not be hard and cracking.

TO PRESERVE THE TOMATOES:

Use traditional Kilner jars and sterilize them first using one of the methods described on page 145.

When you are satisfied that the jars are clean and dry, pack your tomatoes into them and add peeled garlic cloves and sprigs of fresh herbs, such as thyme, rosemary and bay leaves. Pour over extra virgin (cold-pressed) olive oil, making sure that the tomatoes are completely covered with the oil. Cover and seal the jars.

Preserved tomatoes will keep for months and not only do they taste good, they look very pretty on your shelves and will be a great source of satisfaction – which is a lovely side effect of preserving generally.

You can oven-dry most things – try courgettes, aubergines or mushrooms. Fruit, too, dries really well – try peaches and apricots. Indeed, the drying process concentrates the delicious flavours of these organically grown foods.

Opposite: Oven-dried tomatoes can be used to fill sandwiches and bruschetta, in sauces for pasta, or to enrich casseroles. They are especially good on top of home-made focaccia bread.

PRESERVING IN OIL

While northern Europeans traditionally preserved food in animal fat, southern Europeans have always favoured olive oil as a sealant. You might find an estate-bottled, cold-pressed olive oil is a bit strong tasting, so use a good quality virgin olive oil instead. For the difference between oils, read the storecupboard information (see page 15).

One of my very favourite books is called quite simply *Preserving* and is written by Oded Schwartz. He has a recipe for a home-made soft cheese called *labna* which is made from yoghurt but is similar to a cheese we make from sour milk (see page 152). Char-grilled vegetables preserved in oil bring a taste of summer to the winter menu.

CHAR-GRILLED VEGETABLES PRESERVED IN OLIVE OIL

Take 900g (2lb) 'Mediterranean vegetables', such as aubergines, courgettes, peppers, garlic and onions. Cut the aubergines and courgettes lengthways into thick slices, place them in a colander with a large sprinkling of salt and leave to drain for 1 hour before running them under the cold tap and drying them off with absorbent kitchen paper. Deseed and thickly slice the peppers, peel the garlic cloves and peel and quarter the onions.

Place all the prepared vegetables onto a chargrill (ridged grill pan) or griddle pan, brush with olive oil and cook over a high heat for about 5 minutes, turning occasionally, until lightly charred and blistered. If you do not have a chargrill or griddle pan, you can cook these vegetables under a hot grill. Mix the finely grated zest and juice of 4 lemons in a large bowl, add the chargrilled vegetables, stir to mix, cover and leave to marinade for 1 hour.

Meanwhile sterilize a 2 litre (3½ pint) kilner jar (see page 145). Strain the marinated chargrilled vegetables,

Left: Bottled fruit and vegetables. Opposite: The Moroccans preserve lemons in salt, making them less acidic: gently open out the lemons in four segments and sprinkle a teaspoon of salt inside. Close them again and leave to stand for 2 days. Pack tightly into a sterilized jar and cover with half lemon juice and half boiling water, thyme and allspice. Pour a thin layer of oil on top, seal and put aside for 3-4 weeks.

SAVOURY JAMS AND SALSAS

These sweet and sour jams and salsas are delicious. They introduce a touch of the exotic into everyday meals, adding hints of other cultures and providing zesty, hot and piquant flavours.

SWEET CHILLI JAM

This jam has it all — hot and spicy, sweet and savoury. Use it to jazz up sandwiches or to serve with cold meats and fish cakes. In fact, it's so addictive, that you'll be surprised how many things you will find to eat with it! We use fresh red chillies to give the jam a deep jewel-like colour, but green chillies will do just as well.

This recipe yields about 225g (8oz) of this hot jam — use sparingly, it is hot!

  2 cloves garlic, chopped
  5cm (2in) piece fresh root ginger, peeled and grated
  3 small fresh red chillies, deseeded
    and roughly chopped
  225g (8oz) tomatoes, skinned and chopped
    (or use 225g/8oz can chopped tomatoes)
  1 teaspoon vegetable bouillon powder
  50ml (2fl oz) cider vinegar
  150g (5½oz) soft brown sugar

Place the garlic, ginger, chillies, tomatoes and bouillon powder in a blender or food processor and blend to a smooth purée.

Place the purée in a pan and stir in the vinegar and sugar. Bring to the boil, then reduce the heat and simmer for about 30 minutes until thick, stirring occasionally.

Cool slightly before pouring into warm, sterilized jars. Cover and seal. If you are not using it immediately, store in a cool, dark place for up to 2 months. Once opened, keep refrigerated and use within 2 weeks.

GRAPE CHUTNEY

Devised by our head chef Issa Cissokho, we serve this with our Goat's Cheese and Parmesan Tart (see page 64).

This recipe will yield about 1.6kg (3½lb) chutney
  450g (1lb) onions, roughly chopped
  900g (2lb) seedless grapes
  225g (8oz) raisins
  425ml (¾ pint) cider vinegar
  280g (10oz) brown sugar
  2 teaspoons salt
  1 teaspoon ground cinnamon
  1 teaspoon ground ginger
  1 teaspoon saffron strands

Place the onions, grapes and raisins in a preserving pan or large, heavy-based saucepan. Add the vinegar, bring to the boil, then reduce the heat and simmer for about 10 minutes, stirring occasionally.

Above: Grape Chutney adds the finishing touch to Goat's Cheese and Parmesan Tart (see page 64).
Opposite: Sweet Chilli Jam livens up a lunchtime snack.

Add the sugar and stir until it has dissolved. Simmer for a further 20 minutes until the mixture thickens, stirring occasionally. Stir in the salt and spices and cook for a further 5 minutes, stirring. Pour into hot, sterilized jars, cover and seal.

This chutney will mature within 1 month, if you can wait that long, and it will keep in a cool, dark place for up to 1 year. Once opened, keep refrigerated and use within 2 weeks.

SWEET ONION MARMALADE

Use this onion marmalade to sweeten up savoury dishes. It is excellent as an accompaniment to meat, perfect on top of goat's cheese crostini, served on its own with crackers, or in little pastry cases as appetizers.

This recipe yields about 900g (2lb) marmalade.

900g (2lb) onions
2½ teaspoons sea salt
800g (1lb 12oz) brown sugar
100ml (3½ fl oz) balsamic vinegar
50ml (2fl oz) cider vinegar
½ teaspoon ground cinnamon
½ teaspoon ground cloves

Peel and slice the onions into thin rings, then place them in a colander and sprinkle with salt. Mix in the salt, then set aside and leave to stand for about 1 hour. Rinse thoroughly, then pat dry using absorbent kitchen paper.

Place the onions, sugar, vinegars and ground spices into a preserving pan or large, heavy-based saucepan and bring to the boil. Reduce the heat and simmer gently, uncovered, for about 2 hours until the syrup is thick and the onions are golden brown, stirring frequently.

Remove from the heat and leave to cool for 5 minutes. Use immediately or ladle into hot, sterilized kilner jars and seal. This marmalade will keep in a cool, dark place for up to 1 year.

SALSA VERDE

For this beautiful green sauce you can substitute the fresh coriander for fresh basil depending on what it is going to accompany. The coriander version goes really well with fish and the basil version is great with Char-grilled Marinated Tofu (see page 60).

SERVES 4

25g (1oz) capers, drained
55g (2oz) onions
3 tablespoons chopped fresh flat-leaf parsley
3 tablespoons chopped fresh basil or coriander
150ml (¼ pint) extra virgin olive oil
50ml (2fl oz) cider vinegar or lemon juice
sea salt and freshly ground black pepper

Finely chop the capers and onions, either by hand or in a food processor. Place in a bowl, add the chopped herbs, oil, vinegar or lemon juice and seasoning and mix well. Serve immediately or cover and set aside until ready to serve. This sauce will keep in a covered container for up to 24 hours.

SPICY TOMATO SALSA

SERVES 4

450g (1lb) ripe tomatoes, skinned, deseeded and finely chopped (you cannot use canned tomatoes for this recipe)
1 small red onion, finely chopped
1 clove garlic, crushed
1 small fresh red chilli, deseeded and finely chopped
1 tablespoon chopped fresh parsley
1 tablespoon chopped fresh coriander
150ml (¼ pint) extra virgin olive oil
50ml (2fl oz) cider vinegar or lemon juice
sea salt and freshly ground black pepper

Opposite: Salsa Verde

Mix all the ingredients together in a bowl, stirring well, then taste and adjust the seasoning. The salsa is ready to serve. You can prepare this in advance and keep it covered and stored in the refrigerator. Do not keep it for longer than 24 hours or the tomatoes will go soggy.

To make a red salsa which is not hot, simply replace the chilli with a deseeded, finely chopped red pepper.

SWEET FRUIT JAMS AND CORDIALS

These jams and cordials with their vibrant colours bring a taste of sunshine to winter days and evoke memories of berry-picking during the lazy days of summer.

FREEZER JAM

This jam is a favourite of my Canadian sister-in-law, Dee-Dee, and can be made with any soft fruit – strawberries, raspberries, blackberries, blueberries, redcurrants and blackcurrants. It retains maximum taste and nutrition because it has not been cooked. This recipe makes a runny jam; if you want to make it firmer you will need to add extra pectin. We use liquid fruit pectin which is available in most good grocers. Just follow the manufacturer's instructions.

This recipe yields about 375g (13oz) jam
  225g (8oz) fresh fruit (strawberries, raspberries, blackberries, blueberries, redcurrants, blackcurrants)
  375g (13oz) brown or white granulated sugar
  2 tablespoons lemon juice
  liquid fruit pectin (see manufacturer's instructions for quantity guide – approx. 1 pouch to 225g/8oz fruit)

Wash, rinse and sterilize plastic containers or glass jars with tight fitting lids (see instructions on page 145). Each container should be no larger than 225g (8oz). Prepare the fruit by removing and discarding any stems, then place the fruit in a bowl and crush the ripe berries thoroughly using a potato masher or fork.

Left: This cordial is delicious served topped up with sparkling water, or simply serve it as a syrup on top of ice cream or in trifles.
Opposite: Freezer Jam

Layer the crushed fruit and sugar together in a bowl making a total of 4 layers and leave to stand for 10 minutes. Stir in the lemon juice and liquid fruit pectin and continue to stir for about 3 minutes, until most of the sugar has dissolved – a few sugar crystals will remain.

Pour into the prepared jars, leaving a 5mm (¼ in) space at the top of each jar to allow for expansion during freezing. Cover and leave the jars to stand at room temperature until set – this could take up to 24 hours.

You can store this jam in the freezer for up to 1 year. It will keep in the refrigerator, covered, for up to 3 weeks. Defrost the frozen jam at room temperature (allow about 1 hour for the jam to soften) then store in the refrigerator.

DRIED APRICOT
AND ALMOND JAM

This is a lush, perfumed jam. For extra pizzazz add a teaspoon of brandy to every 225g (8oz) jam.

This recipe yields about 450g (1lb) jam

> 450g (1lb) dried apricots (choose organic, non-sulphurized apricots)
>
> 1 vanilla pod, split in half lengthways, or 1 teaspoon vanilla extract
>
> 1 cinnamon stick, or 1 teaspoon ground cinnamon
>
> finely grated zest and juice of 2 lemons
>
> 115g (4oz) brown sugar
>
> 55g (2oz) flaked almonds

Sterilize the jam jars (see instructions on page 145) – use either two 225g (8oz) jars or four 115g (4oz) jars. Place the apricots in a bowl, pour over 600ml (1 pint) hot water, set aside and leave to soak for several hours. Drain and reserve the apricots and soaking water separately.

Place the apricots, vanilla, cinnamon, lemon zest and juice and reserved apricot soaking water in a preserving

Above right: Sieving soft fruit to make a cordial.
Opposite: Dried Apricot and Almond Jam

pan or large, heavy-based saucepan. Add 600ml (1 pint) water and stir to mix. Bring to the boil, then reduce the heat and simmer for about 10 minutes, stirring from time to time, until the fruit is soft.

Add the sugar, stirring until dissolved, then bring to the boil, reduce the heat and simmer for a further 20 minutes, stirring all the time. When the jam is setting (to test, spoon a little jam onto a cold saucer, allow to cool a little, then push a finger across the preserve and if the surface wrinkles and is beginning to set, the jam is ready), remove and discard the vanilla pod and cinnamon stick, if using.

Remove the pan from the heat and allow to cool for 15 minutes. Stir in the almonds, then pour the jam into the sterilized jars, cover and seal. Store in a cool, dark place for up to 1 year. Once opened, store in the refrigerator for up to 2 weeks.

CORDIALS
OR FRUIT SYRUPS

Another wonderful way to preserve soft fruit is, of course, the ancient art of cordial making. This can be done in two ways: the hot method or the cold method. The hot method is easier, but does not produce the same intensity of flavour as the cold. I have included both methods below.

> 900g (2lb) soft fruit, such as blackberries, blackcurrants,raspberries, strawberries, loganberries – either just one type of fruit or a mixture of two or more fruits
>
> 400g (14oz) granulated sugar

COLD METHOD

For the cold method, purée your chosen fruit in a blender or food processor, or mash well by hand. Transfer to a bowl, cover and leave to stand for about 24 hours. Pour the mixture into a sterilized jelly bag (you can buy these muslin bags suspended from a small frame or for small amounts you can make your own by lining a sieve with a double layer of sterilized muslin and suspending it over a large saucepan). Leave for a few hours until it stops dripping.

Measure the juice which should be about 450ml (16fl oz), pour it into a bowl and add the sugar. If the juice does not measure this, add proportionally less sugar. Stir well until the sugar has dissolved. Your cordial is now ready to use, or to bottle, cork and seal, as you wish. This cordial will keep in a cool, dark place for up to 1 year.

HOT METHOD

Place the fruit and 90ml (3fl oz) water in a pan and cook gently, until the fruit is soft, stirring all the time. Pour into a sterilized jelly bag (see instructions above) and leave for a few hours, or until it stops dripping.

Squeeze the bag to extract as much liquid as possible. This should give you about 450ml (16fl oz) of juice – if not, add enough water to make it up to this amount. Pour the juice into a pan and add the sugar.

Bring slowly to the boil, stirring, and skim off and discard any froth from the surface. Boil for about 4-5 minutes, stirring. Use immediately or pour into hot sterilized bottles and cork. Allow to cool, then seal with wax. This cordial will keep in a cool, dark place for up to 1 year.

STORAGE

If you want to store the cordial for a long period of time – which could be up to 1 year with both the hot and cold methods – then pour the syrup into sterilized bottles and fill them to within 5cm (2in) of the top. Soak the corks in hot water for a few minutes, then push them about 5mm (½in) into the top of the bottles. When the bottles are cold, tap the corks further in to make them level with the top of the bottles. Dip the tops of the bottles several times into melted candle wax, allowing the wax to set between applications. Store in a cool, dark place.

Opposite: Soft fruits such as blackberries, blackcurrants, raspberries and strawberries make excellent cordials.

MUSTARDS AND KETCHUPS

Sadly, most people use mustards and ketchups to enliven a bland meal or even disguise an inferior one. Ours are intended to enhance not obliterate and are great additions to grills, brunches and sandwiches.

CHILLI GARLIC MUSTARD

There are two types of mustard seeds, a 'black' seed which is actually brown and a 'white' seed which is actually yellow. The black mustard seed is much smaller and more pungent than the white. White mustard has almost no oil, therefore dry mustard is usually a combination of them both. True Dijon mustard uses the black seed alone and white mustard seed is used in pickles and relishes. Add mustard to a salad dressing and it will help to hold the oil and vinegar together as well as adding delicious flavour. It can also minimize the possibility of curdling when used in a hollandaise sauce.

Makes about 225g (8oz) mustard

- 600ml (1 pint) dry white wine
- 1 large onion, chopped
- 3 cloves garlic, crushed
- 140g (5oz) dry mustard, obtained by grinding half each of black and white mustard seeds
- 3 tablespoons clear runny honey
- 1 tablespoon olive oil
- 2 teaspoons chilli powder or finely chopped, deseeded fresh hot red chillies
- 2 teaspoons salt

Place the wine, onion and garlic in a saucepan, bring to the boil, then reduce the heat and simmer for 5 minutes, stirring occasionally. Remove from the heat and set aside to cool. Strain through a sieve, reserving the liquid and discarding the onion and garlic.

In a bowl, blend the reserved liquid with the dry mustard, stirring constantly, until smooth. Cover and leave to stand overnight.

Blend the honey, oil, chilli powder or chopped chillies and salt into the mustard mixture. Place this mixture in a pan and heat slowly, stirring continuously, until thickened – however, be warned as this will make your eyes water, so keep your head turned away.

Remove from the heat and set aside to cool. Spoon

into one sterilized 225g (8oz) jar or two sterilized 115g (4oz) jars with tight-fitting lids. Cover and seal. Store in a cool, dark place for up to 6 months. Once opened, store in the refrigerator for up to 2 weeks.

If you are interested in making more mustards, there is a good American book called *Gourmet Mustards* by Helene Sawyer.

SPICY TOMATO KETCHUP

This ketchup is a hot favourite with our breakfast eaters. It is slightly spicy, but not so much so that the children won't love it. In any event, the chilli is optional, so you can just leave it out if you prefer. Or, conversely, make it hotter by adding more chillies.

Makes about 850ml (1½ pints) ketchup
   two 200g (7oz) cans tomato purée
   225ml (8fl oz) cider vinegar
   2 onions, chopped
   1 large potato, diced
   55g (2oz) fresh root ginger, peeled
      and roughly chopped
   2 sticks celery, chopped
   1 fresh red chilli, deseeded and chopped
      or 1 teaspoon cayenne pepper
   4 cloves garlic, peeled
   1 teaspoon ground cinnamon
   1 teaspoon ground cloves
   2 teaspoons fine sea salt
   1 teaspoon freshly ground black pepper
   115g (4oz) brown sugar

Place all the ingredients, except the sugar, in a blender or food processor and blend until smooth and well mixed. Pour into a large saucepan and bring to the boil, then reduce the heat and simmer, uncovered, for 30 minutes, stirring occasionally.

Right and Left: Spicy Tomato Ketchup

Stir in the sugar, then bring back to the boil, stirring frequently. Reduce the heat and simmer until the liquid is reduced and thick, stirring occasionally – this will take at least 1 hour. Remove the pan from the heat, cool slightly, then bottle and seal.

If you are bottling the ketchup, first sterilize the ketchup bottles and lids or corks (see page 145), then fill the bottles and seal. The bottled ketchup will keep in a cool, dark place for up to 1 year. If you are making it for immediate use, it will keep in a covered container in the fridge for up to 1 week.

SPICY PLUM KETCHUP

Our plum ketchup is even more popular than our tomato, but it is a seasonal sauce and we can never make enough to last the whole year!

Makes about 1 litre (1¾ pints) ketchup
2kg (4½ lb) plums, washed and stoned
450g (1lb) onions, chopped
55g (2oz) fresh root ginger, peeled
2 cloves garlic, peeled
225ml (8fl oz) cider vinegar
2 teaspoons fine sea salt
2 teaspoons white mustard seeds, ground
2 teaspoons allspice berries, ground
2 dried chillies, ground
10 black peppercorns, ground
115g (4oz) brown sugar

Place the plums, onions, ginger and garlic in a blender or food processor and blend until smooth, then place in a saucepan. Stir in the vinegar, salt and ground spices and bring to the boil, stirring occasionally. Reduce the heat and simmer for 30 minutes, stirring occasionally.

Stir in the sugar, then continue to simmer until the mixture is reduced by half and is thick, stirring occasionally – this will take about 1 hour. Remove from the heat, cool slightly and bottle while hot.

If you are bottling the ketchup, first sterilize the ketchup bottles and lids or corks (see page 145), then fill the bottles and seal. If you are not bottling this ketchup, it will keep in a covered container in the fridge for up to 1 week. The bottled ketchup will keep in a cool, dark place for up to 1 year.

SAGE IN CLARET

Here is an interesting idea for enhancing gravy, which I found in a favourite old recipe book of mine *Plats du Jour* by Patience Gray and Primrose Boyd.

'2oz green sage leaves, 1oz fresh lemon peel, pared thinly, 1oz salt, a pinch of cayenne pepper and a few drops of citric acid (obtainable from chemists) are steeped for 14 days in a pint of claret. The bottle is shaken every day. After this period, the contents of the bottle should be allowed to settle, when the infusion is then decanted into a clean bottle and tightly corked. This can be used to add to the juices of roast pork, duck or goose when the fat has been poured off, to make a gravy, or as an addition to veal goulash or to an onion sauce for haricot beans.'

HOME-MADE VERMOUTH

This is a trick I learned in Spain. Peel oranges (2 per bottle) so that the peel comes away in one lovely looping piece and hang to dry for at least 2 weeks. Collect your bottle ends of red wine in a large jar with a lid. When you have enough wine for a bottle or two, place the dried orange peel in a wine bottle with brown sugar to taste and pour in the wine. Cork and leave to stand for a minimum of 2 weeks until the wine has soaked up the taste of the orange peel and the sugar has replaced the taste of vinegar. Serve and enjoy!

Why eat Organic?

The term organic is applied to all food grown naturally, without the use of synthetic chemicals during any stage of its growing, harvesting and preparation. Animals reared for meat and dairy produce are covered by the same rules as fruit and vegetables: all must be grown as nature intended.

As food producers, the Organic Café is certified by the Soil Association and all our suppliers must also be accredited by a recognized body. In the United Kingdom, organic farmers are bound by the rules of the several recognised certification bodies (see page 186), all of whom are accountable to the national standards organisation known as UKROFS (UK Register of Organic Food Standards).

So everyone who is certified organic is regularly inspected and the chain of supply is carefully checked at every stage – from the farm, through harvesting, transport, storage, processing and retailing. It's a very careful process designed to ensure that organic food really is organic. And the reason that this is crucially important to us and our customers is quite simple. It is because most of the food eaten in this country and in the rest of the developed world is grown with the use of chemicals – often very dangerous chemicals, such as pesticides and herbicides – which pose a threat to our own health and to the health of the countryside.

PESTICIDES ARE POISONS

Pesticides are designed to kill insects, fungi, weeds and small animals, or to prolong the storage life of food and keep it free of blemishes. They are, by design, a menace to all forms of life. Yet pesticides are everywhere. Our farms are drenched with herbicides, fungicides, insecticides and other forms of pesticides and they get into the food we eat, the air we breathe and the water we drink.

Pesticide residues have been found at levels harmful to health in more than a third of the fruit and vegetables sold in supermarkets and shops in Britain. We still do not fully understand the effect of these various poisons but we do know that the effect can be magnified by the human body when we consume a cocktail of them in different foods.

The sheer irresponsibility with which these dangerous chemicals are used in the natural environment is almost beyond telling. In the UK alone, 400 active pesticide ingredients are approved for use and 3,000 different brands are on sale made from these ingredients. Worldwide, there are 50,000 different pesticide brands, and each year about one pound in weight of all these lethal substances is applied to crops for every man, woman and child alive on the planet.

And yet, almost nothing is known about the long-term risks from exposure to these chemicals – and what we do know is all bad. Take Lindane, for example, a widely-used pesticide which has been linked to breast cancer. Yet in 1998, the Soil Association reported that no less than 400 tonnes of this potential carcinogen was applied to UK crops. In Lincolnshire, where Lindane is used extensively on the sugar beet crop, the incidence of breast cancer is 40 per cent higher than the national average. Is this a coincidence?

Pesticides contaminate our drinking water, too. Rain or irrigation water washes them off the crops and into streams and rivers, or carries them down deep into the underground aquifers from which much of our water supply comes. In California, for example, around 1500 wells were declared unsafe in 1990 because of contamination by a pesticide which had been banned 10 years earlier, after links were made to birth defects, male sterility and some forms of cancer. The pesticide had not been broken down by micro-organisms or filtered out by the soil, as the scientists believed would happen. It was still there.

It really is a horror story – and perhaps the greatest horror of all is that our children are particularly exposed to the dangers. This is because their small bodies are less able to eliminate these poisons than those of adults – and also because children eat and drink large quantities of pesticide-treated produce (such as apple juice or grape juice) and so are exposed to higher risks from multiple residues of chemicals.

None of this is necessary. Organic farming methods produce yields as high as those of commercial farms – but without any of the risks, as many studies have shown, including one conducted on Prince Charles's estate at Highgrove.

ORGANIC FARMS

On organic farms, insects, pests and weeds are controlled by natural methods, such as encouraging predators (ladybirds eat aphids, for example) or companion planting. Crop rotation and controlling weeds by traditional methods, such as mechanical harrowing before planting, are also used successfully.

Organic farms do not use artificial fertilizers either, and this is of particular value to the health of the countryside. Artificial fertilizers add nutrients such as nitrogen, phosphorus and potassium (commonly referred to as NPK, their chemical initials) to the soil in vast and unnecessary amounts and they – just like the pesticides – are washed off into watercourses where they pose a threat both to human health and the health of the environment. This problem, too, is avoided by organic farmers and growers, who rotate their crops to preserve the soil's fertility and use natural, organic fertilizers such as compost and farmyard manure to supply nutrients and valuable humus to the soil.

Modern intensive farming methods produce cheap food on a massive scale that is paid for in animal suffering. Most pigs and poultry are reared in cramped and inhumane conditions. Laying chickens are housed in vast tiers of battery cages, or in hangars without windows where egg-laying and meat production can be forced under artificial conditions. The bird's beaks are clipped to prevent aggressive behaviour and there is no possibility of a natural life. The traditional Christmas turkey will have survived stress, overcrowding, suffocation, disease and even brutality before slaughter. Pigs are kept in bunkers on slatted concrete floors. Sows are tethered and crated after giving birth, their only function to give milk to their young from whom they are separated at birth.

Growth-promoting hormones are routinely added to the animals' feed to make them put on weight faster, while antibiotics must also be used routinely because the unnaturally crowded conditions make the animals vulnerable to illness. Needless to say, their feed contains pesticide residues – and all these chemicals (hormones, antibiotics and pesticides) are absorbed into the animal's flesh and passed on for human consumption.

None of these unnatural practices are allowed on organic farms. The animals are reared out of doors – or roam outdoors during the day – and they eat what nature intended. Organically-reared sheep and cattle eat grass, or hay and silage in winter, and all dairy-produce is pure and healthy. Management techniques on organic farms prevent the build-up of disease in the first place but when it does strike, many farms use homoeopathic and herbal remedies in the first instance, resorting to conventional drug treatment only when illnesses are acute. The Soil Association requires that a withdrawal period follows any drug treatment during which time neither the animal nor products derived from it can be sold for eating.

Modern, industrial farming methods also inflict great damage on wildlife and the countryside, ripping up hedgerows and woodland, draining streams and ponds and compacting the soil with heavy tractors and agricultural machinery. It is no exaggeration to say that modern farming is ruining the land, abusing livestock, destroying wildlife and producing food that is unsafe to eat.

So is it any wonder that increasing numbers of people are turning to organic methods and organic food? It is the only form of agriculture that offers a lasting and sustainable future. Less energy is used to produce organic food, too – about half as much as conventional farming, according to a 15-year study carried out at the Rodale Institute in Pennsylvania. So the benefits to the planet from reduced greenhouse gases must also be added to the organic equation.

GENETICALLY MODIFIED FOOD

Genetic engineering is a technology which engineers the transfer of genes from one organism to another, and from one species to another, in order to change the way it behaves. The rules of organic farming prohibit the use of genetically modified (GM) seeds or plants. There is a very good reason for this, because GM foods could pose a real danger to the world. Human health aside, we do not know what effects these artificially-created organisms will have on the environment. Will we be promoting the development of superbugs, resistant to all controls – or

superweeds. Will pests and pathogens acquire immunity – or will our own immune systems be compromised by these genetic experiments?

We do not know the answers to these questions. But we do know one very important thing: the drive to introduce genetically modified foodstuffs is being masterminded by powerful *life sciences* corporations, the same people who produce most of the pesticides currently used around the world. They see the prospect of vast profits from captive markets for seeds and crops which are engineered to tolerate their own patented pesticides.

There are further fears: in a headline case, a leading research scientist was forced into retirement after claiming that laboratory rats fed with GM potatoes had suffered damage to their immune systems and to their internal organs. His claims were backed by 20 international experts; some scientists also believe that genes from GM organisms could spread from crops to contaminate wild plants, irreversibly damaging plant diversity and the wildlife that feed on them.

There is another real threat. These huge corporations hope to win a world market for their products, so that just a few types of engineered crops replace the vast variety of plant and animal foodstuff we now enjoy. This variety is our protection and our pleasure: among the wide range of

potato varieties, for example, are plants with particular flavours and special qualities, such as resistance to cold, to drought or to certain pests. These valuable qualities must be preserved for the future: our food supplies depend on them.

CHEAP FOOD

So organic food and organic farming methods offer a life-saving alternative to the dangerous and destructive practices of modern conventional food production. Of course, organic food may be a little more expensive – but the truth of the matter is that there is no such thing as cheap food. The price is paid in animal suffering, in damage to the land and to the countryside, in pollution and loss of wildlife, and in damage to the health of those who work on the land. So in real terms, 'cheap food' is infinitely more expensive than real food.

But the decisive argument, of course, is that organic food tastes good and does you good. When you buy organic fruit and vegetables, meat, fish and dairy produce, you are getting real value for money – because it is safe and delicious for us and safe and beneficial for the world at large.

So here's to good health for all of us, and a hearty appetite to enjoy organic food!

Organic suppliers

Organic food is no longer hard to come by – supermarkets and wholefood shops are stocking increasingly large ranges that are growing all the time. There are other ways of buying organic products though and one of the most convenient is by mail order – I have listed companies with particular specialities below. For fruit and vegetables, local box schemes are ideal in that they put you the buyer directly in touch with the grower. If you can't find a local scheme I have listed some of the larger ones who are able to deliver further afield. Organic markets and farmers' markets are springing up all over the country offering an opportunity to buy produce that has been carefully raised on a small and sustainable scale. Discovering new sources of good quality produce is half the fun of eating organic – happy hunting!

CHEESE

Many supermarkets now stock organic cheeses such as Lye Cross Cheddar and Brie but for a wider range it is worth checking out the mail order services listed below. These include addresses of both cheese-making farms and specialist shops:

CAERFAI CHEESES
St Davids, Wales
T. 01437 720 548
Make unpasteurized Cheddar, Caerphilly and Caerphilly with leeks and garlic.

THE CHEESE SHOP
Chester
T. 01244 346240
Sells a large range of organic traditionally-made farm cheese, including Staffordshire, Penbryn, Llangloffan, Pencarreg cheeses, Cornish herb, garlic and peppercorn, full-fat soft cow's milk cheese and Acorn organic ewe's milk cheese, either plain or saffron coated.

IAIN MELLIS
Edinburgh and Glasgow
T. 0131 226 6215
They stock between 70 and 80 farm-made cheeses in their Scottish shops. Organic cheeses include Loch Arthur, Staffordshire and Orla Irish sheep's milk cheese.

LLANGLOFFAN FARMHOUSE
Haverfordwest, Wales
T: 01348 891 241
Their own cheese is a rich unpasteurized Cheshire-style cheese made from a mixture of Jersey and Brown Swiss cow's milk. Available plain, flavoured with chives and garlic and as a red Cheshire. Their farm shop also stocks other Welsh cheeses.

Nick samples one of Leon Downey's delicious Llangloffan cheeses for the restaurant cheeseboard.

Carp and pike. As organic farming takes hold and fewer chemical residues are running into our rivers, we can be more confident about eating the fish we catch in them.

LOCH ARTHER
Dumfries, Scotland
T. 01387 760296
The creamery produces a range of organic unpasteurized hard and soft cheeses including an award-winning Cheddar, available plain or with herbs, a small soft cheese called Crannog and a semi-soft cheese called Criffel. They also sell a soft curd cheese and will make up mixed cheese platters and baskets for gifts.

NEAL'S YARD DAIRY
Covent Garden, London WC2
T: 020 7379 7646
Probably the biggest organic cheese store in the country and well worth a visit for any cheese lover. Organic cheeses include St Tola's goat's milk and Orla Irish sheep's milk cheese.

STAFFORDSHIRE ORGANIC
Newcastle-under-Lyme
T. 01782 680366
This cloth-bound unpasteurized Cheddar-style cheese is made both plain and flavoured with fresh herbs, dried herbs or wild garlic.

FISH

Pollution of the rivers and seas and the high use of pesticides in fish farming, make it essential to have some form of accreditation for fish which comes from clean waters and organic fish farms. The following companies can provide these assurances – talk to them about the details.

GRAIG FARM
Powys, Wales
T. 01597 851655
This company import and sell wild fish, caught by dolphin friendly hook and line in clear unpolluted waters off the island of St Helena in the middle of the Atlantic. This fish is the only Soil Association registered wild fish and it is also 'fair-trade produce', with more of the price you pay going to the islanders. The range includes: yellow fin tuna, albacore tuna, grouper, wahoo and mackerel. Graig Farm also sell the first farmed organic trout which comes from Cumbria.

THE ORKNEY SALMON COMPANY
Orkney
T. 01856 876101
The first certified organic fish farm which now supplies supermarkets.

SEVERN & WYE SMOKERY
Gloucestershire
T. 01452 750777
They sell fresh salmon from Glenarm and Clare Island organic fish farms, which are both located in Ireland. They also smoke the salmon in a traditional smokery. They are a good source of wild sea bass, but this is not certified organic.

SUMMER ISLES FOODS
Ross-shire, Scotland
T. 01854 622353
A traditional smokehouse in the far north-west Highlands of Scotland.

They smoke salmon and other fish products which they first marinade in spiced brines with natural ingredients such as rum, molasses, juniper and garlic.

FLOUR

A wide range of organic, traditionally ground flour is available by mail order from several small mills around the country.

DOVES FARM
Berkshire
T. 01488 684880
Large range of stoneground flour and baked products, including spelt flour which is an ancient variety of wheat. Other products include Dove's Farm bread, biscuits and cornflakes – all organically certified.

LITTLE SALKELD WATERMILL
Penrith, Cumbria
T. 01768 881523
A traditional working water-powered mill offering a very wide range of flours and also wheat and rye grain for sprouting. They also run baking courses for the public.

MAUD FOSTER MILL
Boston, Lincs.
T. 01205 352188
All their flours are milled from local organic grain and they produce unusual flours such as maize meal, pancake and chapati flours, together with their own muesli.

N.R.STOATE & SONS
Shaftesbury, Dorset
T. 01747 852475
A 19th-century waterwheel is the primary source of power that drives five pairs of French Burr Mill stones while a Portuguese windmill provides alternative power. Their wide range of flours are all stoneground and their organic flours are available as 100% wholemeal or plain brown.

PERRY COURT FARM
Chartham, Canterbury
T. 01227 738 8449
This is a Rudolf Steiner bio-dynamic farm which produces its own flour. It also has a farm shop and runs a vegetable box scheme.

SHIPTON MILL
Tetbury, Gloucestershire.
T. 01666 505050
A leading speciality bread flour miller whose flours are used by master bakers. They have recently introduced a gluten-free flour and a range of children's baking mixes to encourage children to bake. Their mail order service which is called Flour Direct, offers over twenty specialist flours and includes a contact number for personal bread-baking enquiries.

Nick on a buying trip with Guy Watson of Riverford Farm, one of Britain's leading growers of organic vegetables.

Lizzie and Carol share a joke with Matthew Unwin of Longwood Farm – one of the Café's meat suppliers – at the Portobello Organic Market.

GAME

Organic game must be reared on estates that are certified organic and there are just a few of these. Beyond these, there are many other sources ranging from those where game is raised on land just kept for shooting to those where the game is penned and fed in artificially controlled environments.

HARDWICK ESTATE
Oxfordshire
T. 0118 984 2392
Game is sold from the farm shop on this organic estate along with a wide range of other organic products such as home-made sausages.

BRILLBURY HALL FARM FOOD CO.
Buckinghamshire
T. 01844 238407
In addition to game this farm also raises their own beef, pork, lamb and Light Sussex poultry.

GRAIG FARM
Powys, Wales
T. 01597 851655
They stock local wild venison, wild rabbit and boar, alongside a wealth of other meats and organic products.

GROCERIES

You will increasingly find all you need in your local health food shops or supermarkets, but these people will supply general groceries by mail order:

ABEL & COLE
London
T. 0800 3764040

CERES NATURAL FOODS
Yeovil, Somerset
T. 01935 428791

COUNTRYSIDE WHOLEFOODS
London
T. 020 8363 2933

DAMHEAD ORGANICALLY GROWN FOODS
Edinburgh
T. 0131 445 1490

GREENCITY WHOLEFOODS
Glasgow
T. 0141 554 7633

LONGWOOD FARM
Suffolk
T. 01638 717120

ORGANIC HEALTH
Derbyshire
T. 01773 717718

MEAT AND POULTRY

GRAIG FARM
Powys, Wales
T. 01597 851655
Supplying a wide range of locally produced organic meat, they are the only source of organic mutton. They also produce hand-made pies and pizzas.

HARDWICK ESTATE
Reading
T. 0118 9842392
Beef, pork, lamb, poultry raised on the estate in the farm shop, The Old Dairy. Here they sell a wide range of organic products and in particular their own green top milk and cream.

Christmas is coming ...
and the Hardwick geese
are billed for a starring
role.

HIGHER HACKNELL FARM
Umberleigh, Devon
T. 01769 560909

They supply their South Devon beef and lamb in large quantities and good prices, professionally butchered in a mixed box – all cuts included – for the freezer.

LONGWOOD FARM
Suffolk
T. 01638 717120

Longwood Farm specializes in sausages with the Suffolk, Pork & Herb and Pork & Apple being the favourites. They also rear and sell other meat, including Christmas geese and turkeys. They have stalls at three organic markets in London – Spitalfields on Sunday, Portobello on Thursday and Greenwich on Saturday. They also have a farm shop and an extensive mailing list featuring meat, dairy, fresh produce and bread.

MEAT MATTERS
Wantage, Oxfordshire
T. 01235 762461

Not only do Meat Matters operate an organic meat delivery service, they also deliver organic fruit and vegetable boxes.

Welsh lamb is sweet and tender. Craig Farm in Powys, Wales, has a team of butchers working hard to meet demand.

NATURALLY YOURS
Ely, Cambridge
T 01353 778723
Offer a large range of meat, together with home-made sausages, cooked meat dishes and stir-fry packs.

ORGANIC AND FREE RANGE MEATS LTD
Fife, Scotland
T. 01738 850498
An organic farm since l986, they produce their own meat and also sausages, bacon and haggis.

PURE MEAT DIRECT
Upper Stondon, Bedfordshire
T. 01462 851 5610
Their list of meats includes Eldon Wild Blue Pork, and stuffed meat is a speciality.

SWADDLES GREEN FARM
Somerset
T. 01460 234387
Offering a wide range of meat that has been raised on their own and on colleagues' land in the south west, Swaddles Green Farm also supplies an impressive range of ready-to-eat meals and general groceries.

ORGANIC FOODS LTD
Exeter, Devon
T. 01647 24724
This cooperative venture was set up by a group of organic producers. They can also supply vegetables on request.

SUNDRIES

HAMPERS HAMPERS
London
T. 020 8800 8008
This is a luxury hamper service, containing organic food, wine and chocolates.

THE VILLAGE BAKERY
Melmerby, Cumbria
T. 01768 881515
Bread, pastries, pies, puddings, jams and baking supplies.

PEPPERS BY POST
Dorchester, Dorset
T. 01308 897892
This venture was set up by chilli aficionados and they can supply an exciting range of home-grown fresh chilli peppers and aubergines unavailable anywhere else.

ANGLESEY SEA SALT CO.
Llanfairpwll, Wales
T. 01248 430871
Suppliers of organic sea salt.

HAMBLEDEN HERBS
Milverton, Somerset
T. 01823 401205

Above: Making friends with a handsome Hardwick cockerel.
Right: Potting pepper-coated curd cheese balls.

VEGETABLE BOX SCHEMES

Based on the idea of delivering a box of seasonal organic vegetables to subscribers, box schemes often operate within a small area. To find one near you, see the Soil Association's booklet *Where to Buy Organic* or call the Organic Marketing Company (T. 01531 640819) who have over 120 box schemes all over England. Here is a selection of box schemes that deliver to a reasonably wide area.

SCOTLAND

EAST COAST BOXES
East Lothian
T. 01875 340227

EPO GROWERS
Glasgow
T. 01398 875337

LENSHAW ORGANIC PRODUCE
Aberdeenshire
T.01464 871243

NORTH EAST ENGLAND

BRICKYARD FARM SHOP
Yorkshire
T. 01977 617327

Freshly harvested cabbages from Jenny Usher, a grower and one of the first members of the Soil Association, who sells direct to the public at Spitalfields Organic Market on Sundays.

FIELDGATE
Doncaster
T. 01302 846293
GOOSEMOORGANICS
Leeds
T. 01423 358887
NORTH EAST ORGANIC GROWERS
Northumberland
T. 01665 575785

NORTH WEST ENGLAND
GROWING WITH NATURE
Lancashire
T. 01253 421712
LIMITED RESOURCES
Manchester
T. 0161 226 4777
ORGANIC DIRECT
Liverpool
T. 0151 220 0220
RAMSBOTTOM VICTUALLERS
Ramsbottom
T. 01706 825070

NORTH WALES
DIMENSIONS
Gwynedd
T. 01248 351562
DISCOUNT ORGANICS
Flintshire
T. 01244 881209

SOUTH AND WEST WALES
PUMPKIN SHED
Pembrokeshire
T. 01437 721949

ROGERSWELL
Pembrokeshire
T. 01994 240237
WHITEBROOK ORGANIC GROWERS
Newport
T. 01633 689253

WELSH BORDERS
ABUNDANCE PRODUCE
Herefordshire
T. 01981 540181
GREENLINK ORGANIC FOODS
Worcestershire
T. 01531 640140
SHROPSHIRE HILLS ORGANIC PRODUCE
Shropshire
T. 01588 60735

MIDLANDS
CHEVELSWARDE ORGANIC GROWERS
Leicestershire
T. 01858 575309
NATURAL DELIVERY WHOLEFOODS
Derbyshire
T. 01433 620383
ORGANIC ROUNDABOUT
Birmingham
T. 0121 551 1679
ORGANIC TRAIL
Buckinghamshire
T. 01908 614747
THE ORGANIC WHOLEFOOD NETWORK
Hertfordshire
T. 01923 490526

EAST OF ENGLAND
BLYTON ORGANICS
Lincolnshire
T. 01427 628928
DJ PRODUCE
Suffolk
T. 01638 552709
GREENS ORGANIC FOODS
Norfolk
T. 01379 890199
NATURALLY YOURS
Cambridgeshire
T. 01353 778723
ORGANIC CONNECTIONS INTERNATIONAL
Cambridgeshire
T. 01945 773374
WHEELBARROW FOODS
North Lincolnshire
T. 01469 530721
WOLDS ORGANIC FOODS
Lincolnshire
T. 01507 610686

GREATER LONDON
ABEL & COLE
London
T. 0800 376 4040
FARM-A-ROUND
London
T. 020 8291 3650
THE FRESH FOOD COMPANY
London
T. 020 8969 0351
ORGANICS DIRECT
London
T. 020 7729 2828

A bumper crop of onions from Tolhurst Organic Produce on the Hardwick Estate in Reading.

SOUTH-EAST ENGLAND

ASHURST ORGANICS
E. Sussex
T. 01273 891219

BARCOMBE NURSERIES
E. Sussex
T. 01273 400011

DABBS PLACE ORGANIC FARM
Kent
T. 01474 814333

HARVEST SUPPLIES
E. Sussex
T. 01342 823392

RIPPLE FARM
Kent
T. 01227 730898

SURREY ORGANICS
Surrey
T. 01483 300424

SOUTHERN ENGLAND

GODSHILL ORGANICS
Isle of Wight
T. 01983 840723

NORTHDOWN ORCHARD
Hampshire
T. 01256 771477

ORGANIC LIFE
Berkshire
T. 01628 639054

WEST OF ENGLAND

ARCADIA ORGANICS
Somerset
T. 01934 876886

THE BETTER FOOD COMPANY
Bristol
T. 01275 474545

SLIPSTREAM ORGANICS
Gloucestershire
T. 01242 227273

SOUTH-WEST OF ENGLAND

DARTMOOR DIRECT
Devon
T. 01364 651528

HIGHFIELD FARM SHOP
Devon
T. 01392 876388

RIVERFORD ORGANIC VEGETABLES
Devon
T. 01803 762720

TREGANNICK FARM
Cornwall
T. 01822 833969

ORGANIC MARKETS & FARMER'S MARKETS

For information about when and where these markets are held, contact the Soil Association (see page 158).

WINE AND BEER

AVALON VINEYARD
Somerset
T. 01749 860393
Produces organic wines, cider and fruit wines from their own fruit. By mail order by the case (of no less than ten bottles), plus delivery charge.

CHUDLEIGH VINEYARD
Devon
T. 01626 8533 248
Produces four white wines which are available by the case, including delivery.

DUNKERTON CIDER
Herefordshire
T. 01544 388653
Produces a variety of ciders and perrys available by the case, including delivery.

SEDDLESCOMBE VINEYARD
East Sussex
T. 01580 830715
Produces white wines, cider and apple and pear juice. Mail order catalogue available.

VINCEREMOS WINES AND SPIRITS
Leeds
T. 0113 257 7545
Vinceremos@aol.com
Specialist wine merchant selling a large range of wines, spirits, beers and juices. Mail order catalogue available.

VINTAGE ROOTS
Berkshire
T. 0118 940 1222
Stockists of the largest range of organic wines available in the country. They also supply organic mead and ginger wine together with beers, ciders and fruit juices. Mail order catalogue available.

ORGANIC CERTIFICATION BODIES

Throughout the world there are organizations which monitor and certify organic farmers and growers. Some of these are members of IFOAM (International Federation of Organic Agriculture Movement) and some are regulated by the European Community.

ARGENTINA

ARGENCERT (IFOAM)
Bernardo de Irioyen 760,
17D (1072) Buenos Aires
T. 54 1 334 2943
F. 54 1 331 7185
argencert@interlink.co.ar

AUSTRALIA

NATIONAL ASSOCIATION OF SUSTAINABLE AGRICULTURE AUSTRALIA (NASAA)
PO Box 768, Stirling 5152,
South Australia
T. 61 88 3708455
F. 61 88 3708381

AUSTRIA

SGS, AUSTRIA CONTROLL & CO GES. M.B.H
Johannesgasse 14
A-1010 Wien

Early morning harvesting of leeks for vegetable boxes on Riverford Farm in Devon.

BELGIUM

ECOCERT BELGIUM SPRL/BVBA
Av. de l'Escrime 85 Schermlaan
B-1150 Bruxelles - Brussel
T. 32.10.81.44.94
F. 32.10.81.42.50

BOLIVIA

BOLICERT (IFOAM)
Casilla 13030,
General Gonzales 1317, La Paz
T. & F. 591 2 310846

BRAZIL

INSTITUTO BIODINAMICO (IFOAM)
Caixa Postal 321,
CEP 18603-970 Botucatu SP
T. 55 149 75 9011
F. 55 148 22 5066

FINLAND

NATIONAL FOOD ADMINISTRATION
P.O.Box 111
FIN - 32201 LOIMAA
T. 358-2-760561
F. 358-9-7726 7666

FRANCE

ECOCERT S.A.R.L
B.P. 47
32600 L'Isle Jourdain
T. 33-5-62-07 34 24

GERMANY

NATURLAND-VERBAND (IFOAM)
Kleinhaderner Weg 1, 82166
Grafelfing
T. 49 89 8545071
F. 49 89 855974
Naturland.Germany@t-online.de

GREECE

ASSOCIATION OF ECOLOGICAL AGRICULTURE OF GREECE (SOYE)
26, Averof Str, GR - 10433 Athens
T. 01-8234826

HOLLAND

SKAL
Stationsplein 5, Postbus 384,
8000 AJ ZWOLLE
T. 31/38.42.68181
F. 31/38.42.13.063

ICELAND

VISTFRAEDISTOFAN
Lifraen Islensk Vottun,
Saevarhofda 4, 112 Reykjavik

IRELAND

IRISH ORGANIC FARMERS AND GROWERS ASSOCIATION
56 Blessington Street, Dublin 7
T. 00 353 18307996
F. 00 353 18300925

ITALY

BIOAGRICOOP SCRL (IFOAM)
Via Fucini 10, 10-40033,
Caselecchio di Reno (BO)
T. 39 0 51 6130512
F. 39 0 51 6130224
bioagric@iperbole.bologna.it

LUXEMBOURG

ADMINISTRATION DES SERVICE TECHNIQUES DE L'AGRICULTURE
PO Box 1904, L-1019
Luxembourg

NEW ZEALAND

BIO-GRO NEW ZEALAND (IFOAM)
PO Box 9693 Marion Square,
Wellington 6031
T. 64 4 801 9741
F. 64 4 801 9742
levick@bio-gro.co.nz

NORWAY

NORWEGIAN AGRICULTURAL INSPECTION SERVICE
Post-box 3, 1430

PORTUGAL

SOCERT-PORTUGAL CERTI-FICACAO ECOLOGICA, LDA
Rua Joao de Matos Bilhau,
No 11 loja 13, 2520 Peniche
T. 062-785117
F. 062-785117

SPAIN

DIRECCION GENERAL DE COMERCIALIZACION E INDUSTRIALIZACION AGROALIMENTARIA
Consejeria de Agricultura y Medio
Ambiente, c/Pintor Matias
Moreno, 4, 45002 Toledo
T. 925-266 750
F. 925-266 722

SWEDEN

KRAV (IFOAM)
Box 1940, S-751 49 Uppsala
T. 46 181 00290
F. 46 181 00366
eva.mattsson@krav.se

UNITED KINGDOM

**SOIL ASSOCIATION
CERTIFICATION LTD
(IFOAM)**
Bristol House, 40-56 Victoria
Street, Bristol, BS1 6BY
T. 0117 929 0661/914 2400
F. 0117 925 2504
soilassoc@gn.apc.org

**UKROFS
(THE UNITED KINGDOM
REGISTER OF ORGANIC
FOOD STANDARDS)**
c/o Ministry of Agriculture
Fisheries and Food,
Room G 43, Nobel House,
17 Smith Square, London,
SW1P 3JR
T. 020 7238 5915
F. 020 7238 6148

**ORGANIC
FARMERS AND GROWERS**
50 High Street, Soham, Ely,
Cambridgeshire, CB7 5HF

**BIODYNAMIC
AGRICULTURAL
ASSOCIATION**
The Painswick Inn Project,
Gloucester Street, Stroud
GL5 1QG

T. 01453 759501
F. 01453 759501

UNITED STATES

**CALIFORNIA CERTIFIED
ORGANIC FARMERS
(IFOAM)**
1115 Mission Street, Santa Cruz,
CA 95060
T. 1 408 423 2263
F. 1 408 423 4528
dianeb@ccof.org

OREGON TILTH (IFOAM)
1860 Hawthorne NE, Suite 200,
Salen, Oregon 97303
T. 1 503 378 0690
F. 1 503 378 0809
organic@tilth.org

**ORGANIC GROWERS AND
BUYERS ASSOCIATION
(OGBA) (IFOAM)**
8525 Edinbrook Crossing, Suite 3,
Brooklyn Park, MN 55443
T. 1 612 424 2450
F. 1 612 315 2733
ogba@sprynet.com

USEFUL ADDRESSES

**ENVIRONMENT
AND HEALTH NEWS**
PO Box 1954, Glastonbury,
Somerset BA6 9FE
T. 01603 765670

THE FOOD MAGAZINE
The Food Commission (UK) Ltd,
5-11 Worship Street, London

EC2A 2BH
T. 020 7628 7774

FRIENDS OF THE EARTH
26 Underwood Street,
London N1
T. 020 7490 1555

GREENPEACE
Canonbury Villas, London
N1 2PN
T. 020 7865 8100

**THE HENRY DOUBLEDAY
RESEARCH ASSOCIATION**
Ryton Organic Gardens,
Ryton-on-Dunsmore, Coventry,
CV8 3LG
T. 024 76303517

**INTERNATIONAL
FEDERATION OF
ORGANIC AGRICULTURAL
MOVEMENTS**
Okozentrum Imsbach,
D-66636, Tholey-Theley, Germany
T. 49 6853 5190

THE SOIL ASSOCIATION
Bristol House, 40-56 Victoria
Street, Bristol BS1 6BY
T. 0117 929 0661
F. 0117 925 2504

**WOMAN'S ENVIRONMEN-
TAL NETWORK**
87 Worship Street, London
EC2A 2BE
T. 020 7247 3327
www.gn.apc.org/wen

A cup of fair-traded organic coffee at the Café.

FURTHER READING

E For Additives
Maurice Hanssen, Thorsons, 1987

Environment and Health News
Available from **PO Box 1954,**
Glastonbury, Somerset BA6 9FE
T. 01603 765670

The Food Magazine
Available from **The Food**
Commission (UK) Ltd,
5-11 Worship Street, London
EC2A 2BH
T. 020 7628 7774

The Food We Eat
Joanna Blythman, Penguin, 1996
Go Organic Magazine
Available from **27 Bell Street,**
Reigate, Surrey, RH2 7AD

Healthy Eating for Babies &
Children
Food Commission, Hodder &
Stoughton, 1995

The Organic Directory
Available from **Clive Litchfield,**
Green Earth Books, Foxhole,
Dartington, Totnes, Devon
TQ9 6EB
T. 01803 863260

The Shoppers Guide to
Organic Food
Linda Brown, Fourth Estate,
1998

The Silent Spring
Rachel Carson, Penguin, 1999
(new edition)

What the Doctors Don't
Tell You
Available from **4 Wallace Road,**
London N1 2PG
T. 020 7354 4592

Where to Buy Organic
Available from **The Soil Association**
Bristol House, 40-56 Victoria
Street, Bristol, BS1 6BY
T. 0117 9290661
F. 0117 9252504

Index